SMALL *Oxford* BOOKS

❦

LONDON

❦

Compiled by
BENNY GREEN

Oxford New York
OXFORD UNIVERSITY PRESS
1984

Oxford University Press, Walton Street, Oxford OX2 6DP

London Glasgow New York Toronto
Delhi Bombay Calcutta Madras Karachi
Kuala Lumpur Singapore Hong Kong Tokyo
Nairobi Dar es Salaam Cape Town
Melbourne Auckland

and associated companies in
Beirut Berlin Ibadan Mexico City Nicosia

Oxford is a trade mark of Oxford University Press

Compilation, introduction, and editorial matter
© *Benny Green 1984*

British Library Cataloguing in Publication Data
London.—(Small Oxford Books)
1. London (England)
I. Green, Benny
942.1 DA677
ISBN 0-19-214143-0

Set by New Western Printing Ltd.
Printed in Great Britain by
Hazell Watson & Viney Limited
Aylesbury, Bucks

Introduction

Rome may have been more imposing, Paris more elegant, New York more geometric, Venice more impossible, but there has never been a city remotely like London. Size has something, although not everything, to do with it. In some of the great metropolitan centres of the world it is possible for the longstanding resident to get lost; in London it is impossible for him not to. As the town has swollen, absorbing hundreds of square miles, it has ceased to be a practical proposition for any mind to maintain a comprehensive grasp of the whole. The last man to carry unfragmented inside his head the complete equation of London was almost certainly some unsung neo-Georgian taxi-driver, in the days before philistinism, speculation, and the internal combustion engine conspired so unspeakably to uglify the place.

London is not knowable in the sense that a book is knowable, although it was Henry James who took London to be a giant animated encyclopaedia with people for pages, the most complete anthology of human types in all history. Since James expressed his predictably bookish analogy, London has surrendered its place as the largest, most heavily populated city on the planet. Today, compared to a town like Tokyo, London is hardly populated at all. But greatness is more than a question of statistics. James's analogy of the encyclopaedia was especially apt in one regard, that each of its pages contains new information. London's population, a chauvinist has observed, tells eight million stories; Tokyo's tells one story twenty million times over.

So far as the anthologist is concerned, London's greatest glory is the sheer accumulation of artistic sensibility which has fluttered against its walls. Over the centuries more gifted people have been born into it or been drawn towards it than to any other city in history. They have observed it, described it, celebrated it, used it as an inspirational backcloth for their life's work. Not even the most omniverous reader could digest a tenth of the words expended in London's cause. Its literature is one of those studies which never exhausts itself because there is literally no end to it. Its newspapers and magazines alone could make an anthology a hundred times as fat and, I dare say, a hundred times more readable than the one which the reader presently holds in his hand. Its coroners' reports, its municipal minutes, its architectural or financial or topographical or meteorological notes alone are the stuff of priceless volumes. Above all, the fiction built on the chalk and limestone of London is of so vast a bulk that nobody has ever read it all.

In fact London is two coeval cities, the factual and the fictitious, and there are countless occasions, as the anthologist soon discovers, when the two become inextricably enmeshed. We think of James again, whose first act on arrival was to dash to Ludgate Hill and gaze in awe at the statue on its brow of Queen Anne attended by her handmaidens, excruciatingly conscious even as he gawped that he was imitating the actions of Thackeray's Henry Esmond. In that moment, 'all history appeared to live again', says James, 'and the continuity of things to vibrate through my mind'. James was comically vulnerable to this kind of sentimentality; the very shadows cast by the candle in his room at Morley's Hotel put him in mind, 'I scarce knew why, of the "Ingoldsby Legends"'. We think also of Rose Macaulay, passing childhood afternoons scrutinizing the faces of passers-by in Baker Street, aching for a glimpse of Holmes but finding only a gallimaufry of Watsons. Although none of us is Henry James, how can we, at this late date, contemplate the Hampton Court maze without half-seeing three boatered, blazered young man accompanied by a mongrel dog? How can we pass under the ramparts of the new London Bridge without thinking of the old one, and Gaffer Hexam's grisly angling? Or see the Chelsea skyline without recalling Whistler's ingenious attempts to memorize its crescendos and diminuendos? And yet was Montmorency real, or Whistler imaginary? The literature of London is dangerously seductive. It demands constant vigilance on the reader's part if he is not to end in a delightful swirl of metropolitan impressions which may or may not have actually happened. There is no golden rule, but a useful guide is to assume all the unbelievable things to be real and all the mildly credible ones entirely fictitious.

In some of my selections London is cast as the hero, the central character around whom the supporting cast pirouettes; in others, London is merely the setting, the background supporting an action or an anecdote. Several of the best writers on London have been those provincials who never quite conquered, nor wanted to conquer, their small-town awe of the Big City. Some of the others have been in love, not so much with London as with a part of it, H. M. Tomlinson with Poplar, James Bone with Fleet Street, Wodehouse with Dulwich. Too few of them have composed poems about London. Poetry is a little thin on the ground. I omitted Wordsworth's divine afflatus on Westminster Bridge for the same reason that I omitted the page of pure genius with which Dickens opens *Bleak House*, that both passages occur too often in the anthologies of others to require further duplication in this one.

There are, naturally, the omissions I would rather have avoided. The untypical first-night nerves of W. S. Gilbert, for instance, which caused him to perform the ritual of a trudge along the Embankment until it was time for him to pass through the stage door of the Savoy Theatre and acknowledge the adulation he knew was coming. It is perfectly possible, at least in theory, that on one of these night-walks Gilbert might have bumped into Mr Gladstone, marching the same beat for rather different reasons, looking for fallen women to save. It might have been educational also to have included conflicting reports of London on Armistice Day, 1918. Did perfect strangers really embrace, and go on embracing for hours? We can never know. And what of the Great Plague, Mafeking, the Diamond Jubilee, the 1923 FA Cup Final, King Cholera, Cato Street, Pugin, Bazalgette, Micawber, Pendennis, Peter Pan? They are all part of the history and mythology of London, and their absence from these pages indicates only that they were graceful enough to step down and make way for some slightly less well-known people and incidents.

The scrupulous reader will at last find in this volume the deliberate mistake which I chose not to correct. The mistake is neither mine nor the printer's but the original writer's, the most meticulous, accurate and professional of writers, who yet made a slip regarding one of the most widely-known addresses in world history. I have let it stand to illustrate the fact that sometimes we know something so well that we no longer see it, that the very best of us can be wrong about the simplest things and yet right about every-thing else, and above all because there is something endearing about the mistake itself, as though the town were having a good-natured laugh at the expense of those of us who have been fortunate enough to enjoy a few of its limitless amenities.

Its Primacy

Claims have been made for the primacy of London the extravagance of which are justified only by their accuracy. Experience of London causes a curious shrinkage of our impressions of other cities. As for those born and bred within its limits, they are conditioned to a standard of wit and worldliness which has become the standard antonym to provinciality.

One's first impression is of a heavy city, a place of aching heads. The very name London has tonnage in it. The two syllables are two thumps of the steam hammer, the slow clump-clump of a policeman's feet, the cannoning of shunting engines, or the sound of coal thundering down the holes in the pavements of Victorian terraces.

V. S. Pritchett, *London Perceived*, 1962

London is the only *real* place in the world. The cities turn towards London as young partridges run to their mother. The cities know that they are not real. They are only houses and wharves, and bricks and stucco; only outside. The minds of all men in them, merchants, artists, thinkers, are bent on London. Thither they go as soon as they can. San Francisco thinks London; so does St Petersburg ... The heart of the world is in London, and the cities with the simulacrum of men in them are empty. They are moving images only; stand here, and you are real.

Richard Jefferies, *The Toilers of the Field*, 1892

[1]

It is, no doubt, not the taste of every one, but for the real London-lover the mere immensity of the place is a large part of its savour. A small London would be an abomination, as it fortunately is an impossibility, for the idea and the name are beyond everything an expression of extent and number. Practically, of course, one lives in a quarter, in a plot; but in imagination and by a constant mental act of reference the accommodated haunter enjoys the whole – and it is only of him that I deem it worth while to speak. He fancies himself, as they say, for being a particle in so unequalled an aggregation; and its immeasurable circumference, even though unvisited and lost in smoke, gives him the sense of a social, an intellectual margin. There is a luxury in the knowledge that he may come and go without being noticed, even when his comings and goings have no nefarious end. I don't mean by this that the tongue of London is not a very active member; the tongue of London would indeed be worthy of a chapter by itself. But the eyes which at least in some measure feed its activity are fortunately for the common advantage solicited at any moment by a thousand different objects. If the place is big, everything it contains is certainly not so; but this may at least be said, that if small questions play a part there, they play it without illusions about its importance. There are too many questions, small or great; and each day, as it arrives, leads its children, like a kind of mendicant mother, by the hand. Therefore perhaps the most general characteristic is the absence of insistence. Habits and inclinations flourish and fall, but intensity is never one of them. The spirit of the great city is not analytic, and, as they come up, subjects rarely receive at its hands a treatment drearily earnest or tastelessly thorough. There are not many – of those of which London disposes with the assurance begotten of its large experience – that wouldn't lend themselves to a tenderer manipulation elsewhere. It takes a very great affair, a turn of the Irish screw or a divorce case

Park Lane

lasting many days, to be fully threshed out. The mind of Mayfair, when it aspires to show what it really can do, lives in the hope of a new divorce case, and an indulgent providence – London is positively in certain ways the spoiled child of the world – abundantly recognises this particular aptitude and humours the whim.

Henry James, *English Hours*, 1905

The air seems dead down in this quiet country; we're out of the stream. I must rush up to London to breathe.

George Meredith

A Londoner, who sees fresh faces and yawns at them every day, may smile at the eagerness with which country people expect a visitor. A cockney comes amongst them, and is remembered by his rural entertainers for years after he has left them, and forgotten them, very likely – floated far away from them on the vast London sea. But the islanders remember long after the mariner has sailed away, and can tell you what he said and what he wore, and how he looked and how he laughed. In fine, a new arrival is an event in the country not to be understood by us, who don't, and had rather not, know who lives next door.

W. M. Thackeray, *Pendennis*, 1848–50

It pleased my uncle extremely to find I had never seen London before. He took possession of the metropolis forthwith. 'London, George', he said, 'takes a lot of understanding. It's a great place. Immense. The richest town in the world, the biggest port, the greatest manufacturing town, the Imperial city – the centre of civilisation, the heart of the world! See those sandwich men down there! The third one's hat! Fair treat! You don't see poverty like that in Wimblehurst, George! And many of them high Oxford men, too. Brought down by drink! It's a wonderful place, George – a whirlpool, a maelstrom! whirls you up and whirls you down.'

H. G. Wells, *Tono-Bungay*, 1909

About the London child, reared among the tin cans and cabbage stalks of Drury Lane and Clare Market, there is a breezy insouciance which his country cousin lacks. Years of back-chat with annoyed parents and relatives have cured him of any tendency he may have had towards shyness, with the result that when he requires anything he grabs for it, and when he is amused by any slight peculiarity in the personal appearance of members of the governing classes he finds no difficulty in translating his thoughts into speech.

P. G. Wodehouse, *Lord Emsworth and the Girl Friend*, 1935

Evolving London

There have been several Londons, beginning with the walled city of the Romans, down to the contemporary confusion of bricks, mortar, steel, glass, and concrete. The populations of these succeeding Londons have grown from a few hundreds to a few millions, and there seems to be only one discernible common denominator linking them all. That all-embracing characteristic is fanatical devotion enhanced by the gifts of observation and description.

The citye of London that is to me so dere and sweete, in which I was forth growen; and more kindley love have I to that place than to any other in yerth.

Geoffrey Chaucer

'Nay, but hear me, sweet Sir Harry. Being somewhat late at supper at the Mitre, the doors were shut at my lodging; I knocked at three or four places more; all were a-bed, and fast; inns, taverns, none would give me entertainment. Now, would you have had me despaired, and lain in the streets? No, I bethought me of a trick worth two of that, and presently devised, having at that time a charge of money about me, to be lodged, and safely too.'

'As how, I pray you?'

'Marry, thus: I had knocked my heels against the ground a good while, knew not where to have a bed for love or money. Now what did I, but, spying the watch, went and hit the constable a good souse on the ear, who provided me with a lodging presently.'

Thomas Heywood, *The Wise Woman of Hogsdon*
[Hoxton], 1638

The Great Fire of London, described by a famous eye-witness:

Oh, the miserable and calamitous spectacle! such as haply the world had not seen since the foundation of it, nor can be outdone till the universal conflagration thereof. All the sky was of a fiery aspect, like the top of a burning oven, and the light seen above forty miles round about for many nights. God grant mine eyes may never behold the like, who now saw above 10,000 houses all in one flame! The noise and crackling and thunder of the impetuous flames was like a hideous storm. The clouds also of smoke were dismal, and reached, upon computation, near fifty miles in length. Thus, I left it this afternoon burning, a resemblance of Sodom, or the last day.

John Evelyn, *Diary,* 3 September 1666

When I am in a serious humour, I very often walk by myself in Westminster Abbey, where the gloominess of the place, and the use to which it is applied, with the solemnity of the building, and the condition of the people who lie in it, are apt to fill the mind with a kind of melancholy, or rather thoughtfulness, that is not disagreeable. I yesterday passed a whole afternoon in the churchyard, the cloisters, and the church, amusing myself with the tombstones and the inscriptions that I met with in those several regions of the dead.

Joseph Addison, 'Meditations in Westminster Abbey'

Nothing remarkable happened in our voyage; but I landed with ten sails of apricot-boats at Strand-bridge, after having put in at Nine-elms, and taken in melons, consigned to Mr Cuffe, of that place, to Sarah Sewell and Company, and their stall in Covent Garden. We arrived at Strand-bridge at six of the clock, and were unloading; when the hackney coachmen of the foregoing night took their leave of each other at the Dark-house, to go to bed before the day was too far spent,

Chimney-sweepers passed us by as we made up to the market, and some raillery happened between one of the fruit-wenches and those black men about the Devil and Eve, with allusion to their several professions. I could not believe any place more entertaining than Covent Garden.

Richard Steele, 'A Ramble from Richmond to London'

There was what they call a *ridotto al fresco* at Vauxhall, for which one paid half a guinea, though, except some thousand more lamps and a covered passage all round the garden, which took off from the garden-hood, there was nothing better than on a common night. Mr Conway and I set out from his house at eight o'clock; the tide and torrent of coaches was so prodigious that it was half an hour after nine before we got half-way from Westminster Bridge. We then alighted; and after scrambling under bellies of horses, through wheels, and over posts and rails, we reached the gardens, where there were already many thousand persons. Nothing diverted me but a man in a Turk's dress and two nymphs in masquerade without masks, who sailed amongst the company, and, which was surprising, seemed to surprise nobody ... We walked twice round and were rejoiced to come away, though with the same difficulties as at our entrance; for we found three strings of coaches all along the road, who did not move half a foot in half an hour. There is to be a rival mob in the same way at Ranelagh tomorrow; for the greater the folly and imposition the greater is the crowd. I have suspended the *vestimenta* that were torn off my back to the god of repentance, and shall stay away.

Horace Walpole, Letter to George Montagu, 11 May 1769

1757. – About this period he [Dr Johnson] was offered a living of considerable value in Lincolnshire, if he were inclined to enter into holy orders. It was a rectory in the gift of Mr Langton, the father of his much-valued friend. But he did not accept of it; partly I believe from a conscientious motive, being persuaded that his temper and habits rendered him unfit for that assiduous and familiar instruction of the vulgar and ignorant, which he held to be an essential duty in a clergyman; and partly because his love of a London life was so strong, that he would have thought himself an exile in any other place, particularly if residing in the country.

1763. – Talking of London, he observed, 'Sir, if you wish to have a just notion of the magnitude of this city, you must not be satisfied with seeing its great streets and squares, but must survey the innumerable little lanes and courts. It is not in the showy evolutions of buildings, but in the multiplicity of human habitations which are crowded together, that the wonderful immensity of London consists.' – I have often amused myself with thinking how different a place London is to different people. They, whose narrow minds are contracted to the consideration of some one particular pursuit, view it only through that medium. A politician thinks of it merely as the seat of government in its different departments; a grazier, as a vast market for cattle; a mercantile man, as a place where a prodigious deal of business is done upon 'Change; a dramatick enthusiast, as the grand scene of theatrical entertainments; a man of pleasure, as an assemblage of taverns, and the great emporium for ladies of easy virtue. But the intellectual man is struck with it, as comprehending the whole of human life in all its variety, the contemplation of which is inexhaustible.

1763. – We walked in the evening in Greenwich Park. He asked me, I suppose, by way of trying my disposition, 'Is not this very fine?' Having no exquisite relish of the beauties of Nature, and being more delighted with 'the busy hum of men,' I answered, 'Yes, Sir; but not equal to Fleet-street.' JOHNSON. 'You are right, Sir.'

St. Bride, Fleet Street

1769. – Talking of a London life, he said, 'The happiness of London is not to be conceived but by those who have been in it. I will venture to say, there is more learning and science within the circumference of ten miles from where we now sit, than in all the rest of the kingdom.' BOSWELL. 'The only disadvantage is the great distance at which people live from one another.' JOHNSON. 'Yes, Sir; but that is occasioned by the largeness of it, which is the cause of all the other advantages.' BOSWELL. 'Sometimes I have been in the humour of wishing to retire to a desart.' JOHNSON. 'Sir, you have desart enough in Scotland.'

1777. – I suggested a doubt, that if I were to reside in London, the exquisite zest with which I relished it in occasional visits might go off, and I might grow tired of it. JOHNSON. 'Why, Sir, you find no man, at all intellectual, who is willing to leave London. No, Sir, when a man is tired of London, he is tired of life; for there is in London all that life can afford.'

1778. – I mentioned to him that I had become very weary in a company where I heard not a single intellectual sentence, except that 'a man who had been settled ten years in Minorca was become a much inferior man to what he was in London, because a man's mind grows narrow in a narrow place.' JOHNSON. 'A man's mind grows narrow in a narrow place, whose mind is enlarged only because he has lived in a large place: but what is got by books and thinking is preserved in a narrow place as well as in a large place. A man cannot know modes of life as well in Minorca as in London; but he may study mathematics as well in Minorca.' BOSWELL. 'I don't know, Sir: if you had remained ten years in the Isle of Col, you would not have been the man that you now are.' JOHNSON. 'Yes, Sir, if I had been there from fifteen to twenty-five; but not if from twenty-five to thirty-five.' BOSWELL. 'I own, Sir, the spirits which I have in London make me do every thing with more readiness and vigour. I can talk twice as much in London as any where else.'

J. Boswell, *Life of Johnson*, 1791

... in delectable rooms, which look out (when you stand a tip-toe) over the Thames and Surrey Hills; at the upper end of King's Bench Walks, in the Temple ... I shall be as airy, up four pairs of stairs, as in the country; and in a garden, in the midst of enchanting (more than Mahometan paradise) London, whose dirtiest drab-frequented alley, and her lowest bowing tradesman, I would not exchange for Skiddaw, Helvellyn, etc. O her lamps of a night! her rich goldsmiths, print-shops, toy-shops, mercers, hardwaremen, pastry-cooks, St Paul's Churchyard, the Strand, Exeter Change, Charing Cross, with the man upon a black horse! These are thy gods, O London! ... All the streets and pavements are pure gold, I warrant you. At least, I know an alchemy that turns her mud into that metal – a mind that loves to be at home in crowds.

Charles Lamb

The Metropolitan Explosion

If in the imagination of the modern reader there resides an impression of an archetypal London, then it must be that city which mushroomed in the course of the nineteenth century. At the beginning of that century, London retained many of the properties of a largish country town with an ultra-fashionable heart. By the time the Industrial Revolution and Victorian technology had run their course, its area had multiplied several times over, its population had risen from just over one million to just over five, a new municipal organization, the London County Council, had had to be evolved in a desperate attempt to govern it, and London had become the greatest city in the world, not simply in terms of achievement, or interest, or power, or wealth, but in terms of sheer terrifying vastness. It was the world's first megalopolis, which meant that its Victorian occupants were able to witness change, demolition, rebuilding, growth in a way unimaginable to their ancestors. Before long the London of 1800 appeared in retrospect a lost Arcadian city of dreams.

LONDON SUBURBS

Suburban villas, highway-side retreats,
That dread th'encroachment of our growing
   streets,
Tight boxes, neatly sash'd, and in a blaze
With all a July sun's collected rays,
Delight the citizen, who, gasping there,
Breathes clouds of dust, and calls it country air.

Oh sweet retirement, who would balk the
  thought,
That could afford retirement, or could not?
'Tis such an easy walk, so smooth and straight,
The second milestone from the garden gate;
A step if fair, and, if a shower approach,
You find safe shelter in the next stage-coach.
There, prison'd in a parlour snug and small,
Like bottled wasps upon a southern wall,
The man of bus'ness and his friends compress'd,
Forget their labours, and yet find no rest;
But still 'tis rural – trees are to be seen
From ev'ry window, and the fields are green;
Ducks paddle in the pond before the door,
And what could a remoter scene show more?

William Cowper, from 'Retirement', 1782

In London large quantities of strawberries were grown
in Deptford and Camberwell in the 1830s, and twenty
years later there were market gardens in Bermondsey
and Rotherhithe. A resident of Bow in the 1850s described how it was once 'all fields around' and how
he had been able to see from his bedroom window
twenty-nine church spires. At Leyton people had walked
over cornfields to the church.

Asa Briggs, Victorian Cities, 1963

Grove Lane is a long acclivity, which starts from
Camberwell Green, and after passing a few mean shops,
becomes a road of suburban dwellings. The houses vary
considerably in size and aspect, also in date – with
the result of a certain picturesqueness, enhanced by the
growth of fine trees on either side. Architectural grace
can nowhere be discovered, but the contract-builder of
today has not yet been permitted to work his will; age
and irregularity, even though the edifices be but so
many illustrations of the ungainly, the insipid, and the
frankly hideous, have a pleasanter effect than that of
new streets built to one pattern by the mile. There are

small cottages overgrown with creepers, relics of Camberwell's rusticity; rows of tall and squat dwellings that lie behind grassy plots, railed from the road; larger houses that stand in their own gardens, hidden by walls. Narrow passages connect the Lane with its more formal neighbour Camberwell Grove; on the other side are ways leading towards Denmark Hill, quiet, leafy. From the top of the Lane, where Champion Hill enjoys an aristocratic seclusion, is obtainable a glimpse of open fields and of a wooden horizon southward. It is a neighbourhood in decay, a bit of London which does not keep pace with the times.

George Gissing, *In the Year of Jubilee*, 1894

The pre-eminent master of cockney delineations in the late-Victorian music-hall was Gus Elen (1863–1940), whose art was less sentimentally contrived than Albert Chevalier's, less slapstick than Dan Leno's, and veered closer to genuine character portrayal. Although Elen did not arrive at his cockney stage persona until 1891, the world he reflected in his great songs belonged to the generation before. when working-class London was still a recognizable Dickensian entity. Among those who wrote for him were the lyricist Edgar Bateman and the popular composer George Le Brunn, a gifted musician with a reputation for arriving at the theatre with an insufficiency of band parts; this problem was always solved by a quick tour of all the local public houses between his home and the stage door. In 1899 Elen quickly popularized a Bateman-Le Brunn work which was an authentic item of social history, a folksong masquerading as a joke song:

If you saw my little backyard, 'Wot a pretty
    spot', you'd cry,
It's a picture on a sunny summer day;
Wiv the turnip tops and cabbages wot people
    doesn't buy
I makes it in a Sunday look all gay.

The neighbours finks I grow 'em and you'd
    fancy you're in Kent,
Or at Epsom if you gaze into the mews.
It's a wonder as the landlord doesn't want to
    raise the rent,
Because we've got such nobby distant views.

Oh it really is a wery pretty garden
And Chingford to the eastward could be seen;
Wiv a ladder and some glasses,
You could see to 'Ackney Marshes,
If it wasn't for the 'ouses in between.

We're as countrified as can be wiv a clothes
    prop for a tree,
The tub-stool makes a rustic little stile;
Ev'ry time the bloomin' clock strikes there's a
    cuckoo sings to me,
And I've painted up 'To Leather Lane a mile'.
Wiv tomatoes and wiv radishes wot 'adn't any
    sale,
The backyard looks a puffick mass o' bloom;
And I've made a little beehive wiv some beetles
    in a pail,
And a pitchfork wiv a handle of a broom.

Oh, it really is a wery pretty garden,
And Rve 'Ouse from the cock-loft could be seen:
Where the chickweed man undresses,
To bathe 'mong the watercresses,
If it wasn't for the 'ouses in between.

There's a bunny shares 'is egg-box wiv the
    cross-eyed cock and hen,
Though they 'as got the pip and him the morf;
In a dog's 'ouse on the line-post there was
    pigeons nine or ten,
Till someone took a brick and knocked it orf.
The dustcart though it seldom comes, is just
    like 'arvest 'ome
And we mean to rig a dairy up some'ow;

Put the donkey in the washhouse wiv some
    imitation 'orns,
For we're teaching 'im to moo just like a cah.

Oh it really is a wery pretty garden,
And 'Endon to the westward could be seen;
And by climbing to the chimbley
You could see across to Wembley,
If it wasn't for the 'ouses in between.

Though the gas works isn't wilets, they
    improve the rural scene,
For mountains they would very nicely pass.
There's the mushrooms in the dust-hole with
    the cowcumbers so green,
It only wants a bit o' 'ot-'ouse glass.
I wears this milkman's nightshirt, and I sits
    outside all day,
Like the ploughboy cove what's mizzled o'er
    the Lea,
And when I goes indoors at night they dunno
    what I say,
'Cos my language gets as yokel as can be.

Oh it really is a wery pretty garden,
And soap works from the 'ouse tops could
    be seen.
If I got a rope and pulley
I'd enjoy the breeze more fully
If it wasn't for the 'ouses in between.

Edgar Bateman, 1899

The auctioneer swings his hammer every day in the
homes of the old Sedleys and Veneerings and Surfaces
of our time. Every now and then he opens the door of
a famous house and the crowd comes to gape and get
in the way of the buyers. There is usually some resemblance between these dishevelled, carpetless houses
with their intimate things taken away by the family
and the heavy ornamental objects and bedroom and
kitchen furniture remaining, but a word must be said

about the breaking up of that most hospitable house in London, the bow-fronted old brick house at the corner of Piccadilly and Stratton Street, where the Baroness Burdett-Coutts had lived for three-quarters of a century. At its top corner window Queen Victoria sometimes sat watching like a child the stream of traffic in Piccadilly. 'Yours is the only place where I can go', Queen Victoria said to the Baroness Burdett-Coutts,' to see the traffic without stopping it.'

James Bone, *The London Perambulator*, 1925

Weather Report

One of London's favourite topics of small talk is the weather and its allied themes, light, air, wind, soot, and sky. A peculiar combination of effects embracing climate, pollution and building materials has literally coloured the town in grubby pastel tones more varied than any citizen of a clean city could ever imagine. In the springtime of what other great city would its breakfasting bourgeoisie have been pushed to the extremity of artificial light over breakfast?

It was a cold morning of the early spring, and we sat after breakfast on either side of a cheery fire in the old room in Baker Street. A thick fog rolled down between the lines of dun-coloured houses, and the opposing windows loomed like dark, shapeless blurs, through the heavy yellow wreaths. Our gas was lit, and shone on the white cloth, and glimmer of china and metal, for the table had not been cleared yet.

Sir Arthur Conan Doyle, 'The Copper Beeches', 1892

The voices in the air of unseen busmen and carmen and draymen take on a rounder heartiness excelling their own best efforts when they are visible men, and the policemen loom up in the fog with added grandeur. They require it all, for there is a spirit of misrule abroad; newsboys play tricks and cry strange news, and strait-laced citizens find themselves in public houses, strange companionships are formed, judges and prisoners on bail lose their way and are reported missing at the courts, people go to the wrong theatres,

accidents occur and the ambulance gets lost. Cats come out into busy streets and sit on the pavement as if it was night. Anachronisms like torches and links appear. Only twenty years ago a man going home about midnight in a fog saw a glare of torches and a body of men passed with King Edward walking in the middle. The torches were carried by footmen and policemen; then came the king, heavily wrapped up, with two of his gentlemen; then more policemen; then some stragglers of the night, attracted by curiosity or by the chance of a safe guide to Buckingham Palace. The procession came so silently out of the fog and vanished into it again that the spectator later in the night was not sure that he had not imagined it. But it was King Edward, who had been dining with a Court lady in Portman Square, and, finding it impossible to go by carriage in the fog, had decided to summon torches and a guard and walk just as a Stuart king would have done.

James Bone, *The London Perambulator*, 1925

Wonderfully varied were those seven-and-sixty nights, as he came to remember in after life. There were nights of damp and drizzle, and then thick fogs, beautiful, isolating grey-white veils, turning every yard of pavement into a private room. Grand indeed were those fogs, things to rejoice at mightily. Since then it was no longer a thing for public scorn when two young people hurried along arm in arm, and one could do a thousand impudent, significant things with varying pressure and the fondling of a little hand (a hand in a greatly mended glove of cheap kid). Then indeed one seemed to be nearer that elusive something that threaded it all together. And the dangers of the street corners, the horses looming up suddenly out of the dark, the carters with lanterns on their horses' heads, the street lamps, blurred smoky orange at one's nearest, and vanishing at twenty yards into dim haze, seemed to accentuate the infinite need of protection on the part of a delicate young lady who had already traversed three winters of fogs thornily alone. Moreover, one could come right down the quiet street where she lived, with a delightful sense of enterprise.

The fogs passed all too soon into a hard frost, into nights of starlight and presently moonlight, when the lamps looked hard, flashing like rows of yellow gems, and their reflections and the glare of the shop windows were sharp and frosty, and even the stars hard and bright, snapping noiselessly (if one may say so) instead of twinkling. A jacket trimmed with imitation Astrachan replaced Ethel's lighter coat, and a round cap of Astrachan her hat, and her eyes shone hard and bright, and her forehead was broad and white beneath it. It was exhilarating, but one got home too soon, and so the way from Chelsea to Clapham was lengthened, first into a loop of side streets, and then when the first pulverulent snows told that Christmas was at hand, into a new loop down King's Road, and once even through the Brompton Road and Sloane Street, where the shops were full of decorations and entertaining things.

H. G. Wells, *Love and Mr Lewisham*, 1900

The cries of a London twilight used to oppress him. From the darkening streets and from the twinkling houses inexplicable sounds floated about the air. They had the sadness of church-bells, and like church-bells they could not be located exactly. Michael thought that London was the most melancholy city in the world. Even at Christmas-time, behind all the gaiety and gold of a main road lay the trackless streets that were lit, it seemed, merely by pin-points of gas, so far apart were the lamp-posts, such a small sad circle of pavement did they illuminate. The rest was shadows and glooms and whispers. Even in the jollity of the pantomime and comfortable smell of well-dressed people the thought of the journey home through the rainy evening brooded upon the gayest scene. The going home was sad indeed, as in the farthest corner of the jolting omnibus they jogged through the darkness. The painted board of places and fares used to depress Michael. He could not bear to think of the possibilities opened up by the unknown names beyond Piccadilly Circus. Once in a list of fares he read the word Whitechapel and shivered at the thought that an omnibus could from Whitechapel pass the corner of Carlington Road. The very omnibus had actually come from the place murders were done. Murderers might at this moment be travelling in his company. Michael looked askance at the six nodding travellers who sat opposite, at the fumes of their breath, at their hands clasped round the handles of their umbrellas. There, for all he knew, sat Jack the Ripper.

Compton Mackenzie, *Sinister Street*, 1913

The Broadway lyricist Ira Gershwin (1896–1983) has always been one of the most dedicated and erudite Anglophiles in the American theatre. This affection, nurtured by a love of English literature in general and the works of W. S. Gilbert in particular, was cemented by a lifelong friendship with P. G. Wodehouse, and at last by Ira's visit to London in the 1920s with his composer-brother George in order to supervise the London production of one of their New York successes. The last chore completed by George before his death in 1937 was a Hollywood musical adaptation of an old Wodehouse novel, A Damsel in Distress, in which a Broadway composer arrives in London and falls in love with the daughter of a peer. In the course of writing a declaration-of-love ballad to be sung by the leading man, Fred Astaire, the Gershwins completed a song which soon became famous for its reference to the charm of one of the most famous buildings in London. Later in life Ira was accused of having borrowed the phrase from a letter written to a friend by Isadora Duncan, but years of searching by Ira failed to disclose the supposed reference, which finally tempted him to observe mildly, 'I deserve some of the credit for the phrase too'.

I was a stranger in the city.
Out of town were the people I knew.
I had that feeling of self-pity:
What to do? What to do? What to do?
The outlook was decidedly blue.
But as I walked through the foggy streets alone,
It turned out to be the luckiest day I've known.

A foggy day in London town
Had me low and had me down.
I viewed the morning with alarm.
The British Museum had lost its charm.
How long, I wondered, could this thing last?
But the age of miracles hadn't passed,
For suddenly, I saw you there –
And through foggy London town
The sun was shining everywhere.

Ira Gershwin, 1937

Our Villages

The most hackneyed of all truisms of London life is that the city consists of dozens of boroughs, hundreds of districts, thousands of clearings in the urban jungle whose inhabitants remain so self-contained as to have acquired the comforting insularity of villagers. This is one of the finest of all contradictions of the metropolitan life, that it combines the cynicism of the city slicker with the endearing petty loyalties of the one-horse town. The Belgravia of Oscar Wilde has as little to do with the Dockland of H. M. Tomlinson as Beachcomber's Greenwich does with the comically effete fashionable purlieus of Logan Pearsall Smith.

There is a London for every man in London. London is almost as large as life. There are probably tens of thousands of Jews in Whitechapel who have never seen, or even heard of, Portland Place; there are certainly many people in Portland Place who have vaguely heard of Whitechapel, but only as an outlying territory, like the Andamans or the Solomon Islands, which has to be administered, and may, at any moment, be liable to give trouble. There is a London of the unthinking Rich, bounded on the east by the Savoy and on the west by Kensington High Street. There is a London of the Colonial, a congeries of great hotels and famous 'sights'. There is a London of the stupid American, and a London of the cultivated American, who goes far and wide in search of a background with which his own country does not yet provide him. There is a London of the Chelseaite and the Bloomsburyite; there is a London, frequented and beloved by Mr W. W.

Jacobs and Mr H. M. Tomlinson, and intimately known by Conrad, which begins at Tower Hill and goes eastwards; a marine London, a London of docks, and spars, returned and battered ships, crimps and Chinamen, merchandise and anecdotes from the Seven Seas, tea-chests, bales and anchors, the smells of salt, tar, bilge-water and river-mud. A man knows and loves Acton, but hardly knows where Tottenham is; a man regards Streatham as the secondary centre of the universe, the City being its only superior; and a man lives in Tooting, and finds it difficult to believe that Finchley, with its glitter of trams and shops, exists. Yet for all of them, however widely London may spread, however discrete its parts may become, there is a general awareness of London, and there is a central and nodal part of London which they regard as common property, symptomatic and symbolical of the whole chaotic and magnificent business. In exile they feel it acutely. Wherever the Londoner abroad comes from, it isn't the Balham Town Hall or the Forest Hill Waterworks that most arouses his emotion. After the Union Jack it is Trafalgar Square, or Piccadilly, or St Paul's. It is even possible to imagine a group of British exiles, in the middle of the Gobi Desert, giving, were a sudden picture or wireless message to be encountered, three cheers for the British Museum. London is a hotchpotch but it still has a heart and a soul.

J. C. Squire, *A London Reverie*, 1928

It is a typical City side-street, except that it is shorter, narrower, and dingier than most. At one time it was probably a real thoroughfare, but now only pedestrians can escape at the western end, and they do this by descending the six steps at the corner. For anything larger and less nimble than a pedestrian, Angel Pavement is a *cul de sac*, for all that end, apart from the steps, is blocked up by *Chase & Cohen: Carnival Novelties*, and not even by the front of Chase & Cohen but by their sooty, mouldering, dusty-windowed back.

Chase & Cohen do not believe it is worth while offering Angel Pavement any of their carnival novelties – many of which are given away, with a thirty shilling dinner and dance, in the West End every gala night – and so they turn the other way, not letting Angel Pavement have so much as a glimpse of a pierrot hat or a false nose. Perhaps this is as well, for if the pavementeers could see pierrot hats and false noses every day, there is no telling what might happen.

What you do see there, however, is something quite different. Turning into Angel Pavement from that crazy jumble and jangle of buses, lorries, drays, private cars, and desperate bicycles, the main road, you see on the right, first a nondescript blackened building that is really the side of a shop and a number of offices; then *The Pavement Dining Rooms: R. Ditton, Propr.*, with R. Ditton's usual window display of three cocoanut buns, two oranges, four bottles of cherry cider picturesquely grouped, and if not the boiled ham, the meat-and-potato pie; then a squashed little house or bundle of single offices that is hopelessly to let; and then the bar of the *White Horse*, where you have the choice of any number of mellowed whiskies or fine sparkling ales, to be consumed on or off the premises, and if on, then either publicly or privately. You are now half way down the street, and could easily throw a stone through one of Chase & Cohen's windows, which is precisely what somebody, maddened perhaps by the thought of the Carnival Novelties, has already done. On the other side, the southern side, the left-hand side when you turn in from the outer world, you begin, rather splendidly, with *Dunbury & Co.: Incandescent Gas Fittings*, and two windows almost bright with sample fittings. Then you arrive at *T. Benenden: Tobacconist*, whose window is filled with dummy packets of cigarettes and tobacco that have long ceased even to pretend they have anything better than air in them; though there are also, as witnesses to T. Benenden's enterprise, one or two little bowls of dry and dusty stuff that mutter, in faded letters, 'Our Own Mixture, Cool Sweet Smoking, Why not Try it.' To reach T. Benenden's little counter, you go through the street doorway and then turn through another door on the left. The st irs in front of you – and very dark and dirty they are, too – belong to C. *Warstein: Tailor's Trimmings.* Next to T. Benenden, and C. Warstein is a door, a large, stout, old door from which most of the paint has flaked and shredded away. This door has no name on it, and nobody, not even T. Benenden, has seen it open or knows what there is behind it. There it is, a door, and it does nothing but gather dust and cobwebs and occasionally drop another flake of dried paint on the worn step below. Perhaps it leads into another world. Perhaps it will open, one morning, to admit an angel, who, after looking up and down the little street for a moment, will suddenly blow the last trumpet. Perhaps that is the real reason why the street is called Angel Pavement. What is certain, however, is that this door has no concern with the building next to it and above it, the real neighbour of T. Benenden and C. Warstein and known to the postal authorities as No. 8, Angel Pavement.

No. 8, once a four-storey dwelling-house where some merchant-alderman lived snugly on his East India dividends, is now a little hive of commerce. For the last few years, it has contrived to keep an old lady and a companion (unpaid) in reasonable comfort at The Palms Private Hotel, Torquay, and, in addition, to furnish the old lady's youngest niece with an allowance of two pounds a week in order that she might continue to share a studio just off the Fulham Road and attempt to design scenery for plays that are always about to be produced at the Everyman Theatre, Hampstead. It has also indirectly paid the golf club subscription and caddie fees of the junior partner of Fulton, Gregg and Fulton, the solicitors, who are responsible for the letting and the rents. As for the tenants themselves, their names may be found on each side of the squat doorway. The ground floor is occupied by the *Kwik-Work Razor Blade Co., Ltd.*, the first floor by *Twigg & Dersingham*, and the upper floors by the *Universal Hosiery Co.*, the *London and Counties Supply Stores*, and, at the very top, keeping its eye on everybody, the *National Mercantile Enquiry Agency*, which seems to be content with the possession of a front attic.

This does not mean that we have now finished with No. 8, Angel Pavement. It is for the sake of No. 8 that we have come to Angel Pavement at all, but not for the whole of No. 8, but only for the first floor. No doubt a number of tales, perhaps huge violent epics, could be started, jumped into life, merely by opening the door of the *Kwik-Work Razor Blade Co., Ltd.*, or by trudging up the stairs to the *Universal Hosiery Co.* and the *London and Counties Supply Stores*, or by looking up at the grimy skylight, and giving a shout to the *National Mercantile Enquiry Agency*; but we must keep to the less mysterious but more respectable first floor – and *Twigg & Dersingham*.

J. B. Priestley, *Angel Pavement*, 1930

PARLIAMENT HILL FIELDS

Rumbling under blackened girders, Midland,
    bound for Cricklewood,
Puffed its sulphur to the sunset where that
    Land of Laundries stood.
Rumble under, thunder over, train and tram
    alternate go,
Shake the floor and smudge the ledger,
    Charrington, Sells, Dale and Co.,
Nuts and nuggets in the window, trucks along
    the lines below.

When the Bon Marché was shuttered, when
    the feet were hot and tired,
Outside Charrington's we waited, by the
    'STOP HERE IF REQUIRED',

[26]

Launched aboard the shopping basket, sat
   precipitately down,
Rocked past Zwanziger the baker's, and the
   terrace blackish brown,
And the curious Anglo-Norman parish church
   of Kentish Town.

Till the tram went over thirty, sighting
   terminus again,
Past municipal lawn tennis and the bobble-
   hanging plane;
Soft the light suburban evening caught our
   ashlar-speckled spire,
Eighteen-sixty Early English, as the mighty
   elms retire
Either side of Brookfield Mansions flashing fine
   French-window fire.

Oh the after-tram-ride quiet, when we heard a
   mile beyond,
Silver music from the bandstand, barking dogs
   by Highgate Pond;
Up the hill where stucco houses in Virginia
   creeper drown –
And my childish wave of pity, seeing children
   carrying down
Sheaves of drooping dandelions to the courts of
   Kentish Town.

John Betjeman

*The history of metropolitan homicide is long and
varied, but no transgression in that catalogue is more
comically absurd, or more absurdly comic, than that of
Oscar Wilde's Lord Arthur Savile. At least one biogra-
pher, Hesketh Pearson, has stressed the fact that the
story began its life as a verbal improvisation of Wilde's
which lost something with the transition to the form-
ality of the written word. The published version still
remains ridiculous enough to have diverted generations*

*of readers, besides showing the author's familiarity with
the streets of central London.*

First he came to the Park, whose sombre woodland
seemed to fascinate him. He leaned wearily up against
the railings, cooling his brow against the wet metal,
and listening to the tremulous silence of the trees.
'Murder! murder!' he kept repeating, as though iteration
could dim the horror of the word. The sound of his
own voice made him shudder, yet he almost hoped that
Echo might hear him, and wake the slumbering city
from its dreams. He felt a mad desire to stop the casual
passer-by, and tell him everything.

Then he wandered across Oxford Street into narrow,
shameful alleys. Two women with painted faces mocked
at him as he went by. From a dark courtyard came a
sound of oaths and blows, followed by shrill screams,
and, huddled upon a damp door-step, he saw the
crooked-backed forms of poverty and eld. A strange
pity came over him. Were these children of sin and
misery predestined to their end, as he to his? Were
they, like him, merely the puppets of a monstrous
show?

And yet it was not the mystery, but the comedy of
suffering that struck him; its absolute uselessness, its
grotesque want of meaning. How incoherent everything seemed! How lacking in all harmony! He was
amazed at the discord between the shallow optimism
of the day, and the real facts of existence. He was still
very young.

After a time he found himself in front of Marylebone
Church. The silent roadway looked like a long riband
of polished silver, flecked here and there by the dark
arabesques of waving shadows. Far into the distance
curved the line of flickering gas-lamps, and outside a
little walled-in house stood a solitary hansom, the
driver asleep inside. He walked hastily in the direction
of Portland Place, now and then looking round, as
though he feared that he was being followed. At the

corner of Rich Street stood two men, reading a small
bill upon a hoarding. An odd feeling of curiosity stirred
him, and he crossed over. As he came near, the word
'Murder', printed in black letters, met his eye. He
started, and a deep flush came into his cheek. It was
an advertisement offering a reward for any information
leading to the arrest of a man of medium height,
between thirty and forty years of age, wearing a billy-
cock hat, a black coat, and check trousers, and with a
scar upon his right cheek. He read it over and over
again, and wondered if the wretched man would be
caught, and how he had been scarred. Perhaps, some
day, his own name might be placarded on the walls of
London. Some day, perhaps, a price would be set on
his head also.

The thought made him sick with horror. He turned
on his heel, and hurried on into the night.

Where he went he hardly knew. He had a dim
memory of wandering through a labyrinth of sordid
houses, and it was bright dawn when he found himself
at last in Piccadilly Circus. As he strolled home towards
Belgrave Square, he met the great waggons on their
way to Covent Garden. The white-smocked carters,

with their pleasant sunburnt faces and coarse curly hair, strode sturdily on, cracking their whips, and calling out now and then to each other; on the back of a huge grey horse, the leader of a jangling team, sat a chubby boy, with a bunch of primroses in his battered hat, keeping tight hold of the mane with his little hands, and laughing; and the great piles of vegetables looked like masses of jade against the morning sky, like masses of green jade against the pink petals of some marvellous rose. Lord Arthur felt curiously affected, he could not tell why. There was something in the dawn's delicate loveliness that seemed to him inexpressibly pathetic, and he thought of all the days that break in beauty, and that set in storm. These rustics, too, with their rough, good-humoured voices, and their nonchalant ways, what a strange London they saw! A London free from the sin of night and the smoke of day, a pallid, ghost-like city, a desolate town of tombs! He wondered what they thought of it, and whether they knew anything of its splendour and its shame, of its fierce, fiery-coloured joys, and its horrible hunger, of all it makes and mars from morn to eve. Probably it was to them merely a mart where they brought their fruit to sell, and where they tarried for a few hours at most, leaving the streets still silent, the houses still asleep. It gave him pleasure to watch them as they went by. Rude as they were, with their heavy, hob-nailed shoes, and their awkward gait, they brought a little of Arcady with them. He felt that they had lived with Nature, and that she had taught them peace. He envied them all that they did not know.

By the time he had reached Belgrave Square the sky was a faint blue, and the birds were beginning to twitter in the gardens.

Oscar Wilde, *Lord Arthur Savile's Crime*, 1891

The coffee-room at Morley's was a new scene of amusement to Ferdinand, and he watched with great diversion the two evening papers portioned out among twelve eager quidnuncs, and the evident anxiety which they endured, and the nice diplomacies to which they resorted, to obtain the envied journals. The entrance of our two travellers, so alarmingly increasing the demand over the supply, at first seemed to attract considerable and not very friendly notice; but when a malignant half-pay officer, in order to revenge himself for the restless watchfulness of his neighbour, a political doctor of divinity, offered the journal, which he had long finished, to Glastonbury, and it was declined, the general alarm visibly diminished. Poor Mr Glastonbury had never looked into a newspaper in his life, save the *County Chronicle*, to which he occasionally contributed a communication, giving an account of the digging up of some old coins, signed Antiquarius; or of the exhumation of some fossil remains, to which he more boldly appended his initials.

In spite of the strange clatter in the streets, Ferdinand slept well, and the next morning, after an early breakfast, himself and his fellow-traveller set out on their peregrinations. Young and sanguine, full of health and enjoyment, innocent and happy, it was with difficulty that Ferdinand could restrain his spirits as he mingled in the bustle of the streets. It was a bright sunny morning, and although the end of June, the town was yet quite full.

'Is this Charing Cross, sir? I wonder if we shall ever be able to get over. Is this the fullest part of the town, sir? What a fine day, sir! How lucky we are in the weather! We are lucky in everything! Whose house is that? Northumberland House! Is it the Duke of Northumberland's? Does he live there? How I should like to see it! Is it very fine? Who is that? What is this? The Admiralty; oh, let me see the Admiralty! The Horse Guards! Oh! where, where? Let us set our watches by the Horse Guards. The guard of our coach always sets his watch by the Horse Guards. Mr Glastonbury, which is the best clock, the Horse Guards or

Horse Guards

St Paul's? Is that the Treasury? Can we go in? That is Downing Street, is it? I never heard of Downing Street. What do they do in Downing Street? Is this Charing Cross still, or is it Parliament Street? Where does Charing Cross end, and where does Parliament Street begin? By Jove, I see Westminster Abbey!'

Benjamin Disraeli, *Henrietta Temple*, 1837

'The first thing to do', said Psmith, 'is to ascertain that such a place as Clapham Common really exists. One has heard of it, of course, but has its existence ever been proved? I think not. Having accomplished that, we must then try to find out how to get to it. I should say at a venture that it would necessitate a sea voyage.'

P. G. Wodehouse, *Psmith in the City*, 1910

From my high window in central Dockland, as from a watch tower, I look out over a tumbled waste of roofs and chimneys, a volcanic desert, inhabited only by sparrows and pigeons. Humanity burrows in swarms below that surface of crags, but only faint cries tell me that the rocks are caverned and inhabited, that life flows there unseen through subterranean galleries. Often, when the sunrise over the roofs is certainly the coming of Aurora, as though then the first illumination of the sky heralded the veritable dayspring for which we look, and the gods were nearly here, I have watched for that crust beneath, which seals the sleepers under, to heave and roll, to burst, and for released humanity to pour through fractures, from the lower dark, to be renewed in the fires of the morning. Nothing has happened yet. But I am confident it would repay society to appoint another watcher when I am gone, to keep an eye on the place.

Right below my window there are two ridges running in parallel jags of chimneys, with a crevasse between them to which I can see no bottom. But a roadway is there. From an acute angle of the window a cornice overhangs a sheer fall of cliff. That is as near the ground as can be got from my outlook. Several superior peaks rise out of the wilderness, where the churches are; and beyond the puzzling middle distance, where smoke dissolves all form, loom the dock warehouses, a continuous range of far dark heights. I have thoughts of a venturesome and lonely journey by moonlight, in and out of the chimney stacks, and all the way to the distant mountains. It looks inviting, and possible, by moonlight. And, indeed, any bright day in summer, from my window, Dockland with its goblin-like chimneys might be the enchanted country of a child's dream, where shapes, though inanimate, are watchful and protean.

H. M. Tomlinson, *London River*, 1921

GREENWICH OBSERVATORY

A new nightwatchman, a simple country lad, arrived here some days ago. Things were going on in the sky on the first night of his arrival, and he watched one of the astronomers aiming a gigantic telescope at the heavens. Suddenly a shooting star swung out and fell through space.

'That was a good shot, sir', said the simple lad.

The older men at Greenwich deny the truth of this story.

J. B. Morton, ('Beachcomber') 'Morton's Folly', 1933

Some day I will go to London, and spend a day or two amid the dear old horrors. Some of the places, I know, have disappeared. I see the winding way by which I went from Oxford Street, at the foot of Tottenham Court Road, to Leicester Square, and, somewhere in the labyrinth (I think of it as always foggy and gas-lit) was a shop which had pies and puddings in the window, puddings and pies kept hot by steam rising through the perforated metal. How many a time have I stood there, raging with hunger, unable to purchase even one pennyworth of food! The shop and the street have long since vanished; does any man remember them so feelingly as I? But I think most of my haunts are still in existence: to tread again those pavements, to look at those grimy doorways and purblind windows, would affect me strangely.

I see that alley hidden on the west side of Tottenham Court Road, where, after living in a back bedroom on the top-floor, I had to exchange for the front cellar; there was a difference, if I remember rightly, of sixpence a week, and sixpence, in those days, was a very great consideration – why, it meant a couple of meals. (I once *found* sixpence in the street, and had an exultation which is vivid in me at this moment.) The front cellar was stone-floored; its furniture was a table, a chair, a wash-stand, and a bed; the window, which of course had never been cleaned since it was put in, received light through a flat grating in the alley above. Here I lived; here I *wrote*. Yes, 'literary work' was done at that filthy deal table, on which, by the bye, lay my Homer, my Shakespeare, and the few other books I then possessed. At night, as I lay in bed, I used to hear the tramp, tramp of a *posse* of policemen who passed along the alley on their way to relieve guard; their heavy feet sometimes sounded on the grating above my window.

I recall a tragi-comical incident of life at the British Museum. Once, on going down into the lavatory to wash my hands, I became aware of a notice newly

[34]

set up above the row of basins. It ran somehow thus: 'Readers are requested to bear in mind that these basins are to be used only for casual ablutions.' Oh, the significance of that inscription! Had I not myself, more than once, been glad to use this soap and water more largely than the sense of the authorities contemplated? And there were poor fellows working under the great dome whose need, in this respect, was greater than mine. I laughed heartily at the notice, but it meant so much.

George Gissing, *The Private Papers of Henry Ryecroft*, 1903

REGENT'S PARK TERRACE

The noises round my house. On cobbles bounding
Victorian-fashioned drays laden with railway goods;
their hollow sound like stones in rolling barrels:
the stony hoofing of dray horses.

Further, the trains themselves; among them the
    violent,
screaming like frightened animals, clashing metal;
different the pompous, the heavy breathers, the
    aldermen,
or those again which speed with the declining
sadness of crying along the distant routes
knitting together weathers and dialects.

Between these noises the little teeth
of a London silence.

Finally the lions grumbling over the park,
angry in the night hours,
cavernous as though their throats were openings up
from the earth:
hooves, luggage, engines, tumbrils, lions,
hollow noises, noises of travel, hourly these unpick
the bricks of a London terrace, make the ear
their road, and have their audience in whatever
hearing the heart or the deep of the belly owns.

Bernard Spencer, 1963

It was easy going, downhill from St Paul's to Ludgate
Circus; down hill to hansom cabs dancing, to a jingle
of bells, as if timbrels and castanets accompanied him.
The portico to the west was the railway bridge at the
bottom of the hill, and that cloud of white vapour from
a locomotive, the light mixed with it, was a pillar of
fire above the vista of fabulous Fleet Street. That was
not his street though. Never could be. It was shut
closer than Cheapside. There were many doors in it,
but not one for him. They were only for the elect, to
whom the land was promised at Oxford or Cambridge.
Either you were invited in, without a plea, or you
stayed out. You are always held up, of course, in the
approach to Fleet Street. You are sure to be checked at
Ludgate Circus. The traffic there is against you. Clem
waited to cross, and in that pause another doubt came
to him, as he watched the north and south vans go
past. Fleet Street, very likely, was as bad as Cheapside,
in its special way. What was its special way? Steam
lorries thundered by him to a smell of radiant grease.
Those lorries were a sort of warning. He could read
on them their near destination. They boldly advertised
it. Each lorry was loaded with huge white cylinders of
news-sheet, the popular press for next morning in
embryo. Each lorry carried what had been a balsamic
American pine forest, but the forest was slain, deodor-
ized, pulped, and thinned out into a load of titanic
white rolls, to take Sir Alfred Harmsworth's basic
impressions.

H. M. Tomlinson, *The Day Before*, 1940

It was not bad sport – being in London entirely on our
own hook. We asked the way to Fleet Street, where
father says all the newspaper offices are. They said
straight on down Ludgate Hill – but it turned out to
be quite another way. At least WE didn't go straight
on. We got to St Paul's. Noel would go in, and when
we asked a policeman he said we'd better go back
through Smithfield. So we did. They don't burn people

Fleet Street

any more there now, so it was rather dull, besides
being a long way, and Noel got very tired. He's a
peaky little chap; it comes of being a poet, I think.
We had a bun or two at different shops and it was
quite late in the afternoon when we got to Fleet Street.
The gas was lighted and the electric lights. There is a
jolly Bovril sign that comes off and on in different
coloured lamps. We went to the 'Daily Recorder' office,
and asked to see the Editor. It is a big office, very
bright, with brass and mahogany and electric lights.

They told us the Editor wasn't there, but at another
office. So we went down a dirty street, to a very dull-
looking place. There was a man there inside, in a glass
case, as if he was a museum, and he told us to write
down our names and business.

E. Nesbit, *The Story of the Treasure Seekers*, 1899

In some moods one feels the whole thing is some
owlish and baronial fake from a German barony; in
others, it has that unhappy familiar ugliness for which
we begin to have an affectionate pity, reflecting that it
has what in his literary way the Londoner likes most:
character. People put up with Queen Victoria because
she had that: something preposterous and incurable. In
yet another mood we recover the generous feeling that
familiarity and the weather make the bridge part of

[37]

Nature; and, as I have said before, in the best and the worst sense of the idea, we are infatuated with Nature. London has the art of looking mysteriously sad. Seen through the kindness of fog or mist, the Tower Bridge has the beauty of a heavy web hung from the sky or floating like some ghostly schooner just above the surface of the water. On clear days, the sky stares through it like an imprisoned face; and, in the evening, if you are sitting on the terrace of one of those little seventeenth-century houses, close to the Mayflower in Rotherhithe, the bridge looks spacious and sweeping, springing lightly over the river, which here is wide. The towers and their cantilevers blacken against the evening sky and, if the sky is feathery or the sunset light and yellowish, the bridge is a noble frame for the pigeon-coloured lanterns and belfries of Wren's churches and the dome of St Paul's, resting, dumb as an egg, on its hill.

V. S. Pritchett, *London Perceived*, 1962

The Strand is a withered place to those who remember it in Victorian and Edwardian days when Richard Le Gallienne wrote of it:

> Alight, alight on either hand –
> The iron lilies of the Strand!

and told us how 'like dragon-flies the hansoms hovered'. Phil May often sat in one of them outside Romano's Restaurant and sketched the the Strand crowd, then rumpled with fuzzy old actors, with terrible fur collars on their coats, who called one another 'laddie' and read the 'Pink 'Un', a sporting paper. More marriages, they say, were then made at Romano's, than in heaven as between 'Gaiety girls' and the peerage. Behind Romano's in narrow Maiden Lane is Rule's which preserves in marble sculpture in glassy niches, old prints of players and boxers and Aladdin lampshades and potpourri in Sheffield-plate bowls, the last enchantments of mid-Victoria. The Prince of Wales who became Edward the Seventh in history and Prince Florizel of Bohemia in fiction had little parties there, and Miss Gertrude Lawrence has told in her book how his grandson, the Duke of Windsor, ate his supper there with Thespian friends. Turner, painter of sun and sunrise, was born in the lane almost opposite Rule's; Thackeray's 'Coal Hole' where Colonel Newcome brought young Clive and where Captain Shannon and the other gentlemen of the press took their ease was in that shadowed lane behind the roaring Strand.

Gow's in the Strand was more curious than the grander and many-pewed Simpson's across the way. Gow's was the place where theatrical critics forgathered after a play to eat a sandwich, quaff from a pewter and exchange clichés before going to Fleet Street to write them into their notices in the old leisurely nights before the wars when papers went to press at one. Sala on his return from France, where he had gone to write articles on the cuisine of Paris, cried when he landed at Charing Cross Station, 'Ah, – now for a steak at Gow's!'. It was good English food and cooking there and the waiter upstairs when upbraided about the poorness of the coffee said, 'Well, sir, you see we've got to keep up the reputation of an English house!'

Then there was Gatti's at Charing Cross, established by two Swiss brothers in 1862, which had a clientele and an air of its own. It was the middle-class house for doing yourself well on a night out in London. Elderly people were happy there after their fashion. I think of its long café room, too, as the home of the lonely man. On a Saturday night you would see them, each sitting under a hat tree smoking a meditative cigar, thinking of the old days when supper at Gatti's was an adventure, and of lost friends, and a scattered family, and how it would have been different if the wife had lived. I remember sitting next to one such lonely man on a Derby race night, and he told me he always came to Gatti's on Derby night and ate a steak, drank a pint of bitter and went home to Streatham Hill by a late bus. Always. On Derby nights. He had never been to a race meeting but it made you feel you weren't out of the swim.

Before Britain was in the war, there were strange sights as the Germans and Frenchmen responded to their mobilization orders and departed, most of them from the same station, Charing Cross. The station resounded with national anthems and taunts and curses and farewells. Insults were chalked on carriage doors, yet there were some links to be broken between mates, French and German, who had worked together in stockbrokers' offices, in banks, in hotels, in the press. The French and German waiters in one big Regent Street restaurant, the story went, decided to 'pair' like Parliament men and stay peaceably in London, but in the end the Germans went to detention camps and the French to the war. I noticed at Charing Cross Station that all the Germans wore brand new English boots, a shrewd piece of German mobilization technique. Off they went – German, French and sad-eyed Belgians. 'Deutschland, Deutschland, über alles!' roared from one train; 'Le jour de gloire est arrivé' from the other.

James Bone, *London Echoing*, 1948

*That the contemplation of London is a subjective
exercise was never better demonstrated than by the
contrasting reactions to the same vista by two con-
temporaneous Englishmen. Here is the born pessimist:*

I was walking westward up the Strand, and though it
was coldish I went slowly to get the pleasure of my
cigar. The usual crowd that you can hardly fight your
way through was streaming up the pavement, all of
them with that insane fixed expression on their faces
that people have in London streets, and there was the
usual jam of traffic with the great red buses nosing
their way between the cars, and the engines roaring
and horns tooting. Enough noise to waken the dead,
but not to waken this lot, I thought. I felt as if I was
the only person awake in a city of sleepwalkers.

George Orwell, *Coming Up for Air*, 1939

*But twenty years before, Alpha of the Plough, whose
rustic soubriquet thinly concealed the cheerful urbanity
of the essayist A. G. Gardiner, had strolled through the
same crowds to very different reactions:*

The Strand is to me always the most attractive street
I know, especially on bright afternoons when the sun
is drooping behind the Admiralty Arch and its light
glints and dances in the eyes of the crowd moving
westward. Then it is that I seem to see the wayfarers
transfigured into a procession hurrying in pursuit of
some sunlit adventure of the soul, and am almost
persuaded to turn round and catch with them the flash
of vision that gleams in their eyes.

*But then Gardiner was as resolute in his pursuit of
cheerfulness as Orwell was in his search for glum
despair. Not surprisingly it is Gardiner who evokes the
kindly vision of Samuel Pepys going down to Greenwich
to enjoy himself in the company of that other great
London chronicler, John Evelyn:*

... the receipt of the news of a sea victory did put us all into such an extasy of joy that it inspired into Sir J. Minnes and Mr Evelyn such a spirit of mirth that in all my life I never met so merry a two hours as our company this night. Among other humours, Mr Evelyn's repeating of some verses made up of nothing but the various acceptations of 'may' and 'can', and doing it so aptly upon occasion of something of that nature, and so fast, did make us all die almost with laughing, and did so stop the mouth of Sir J. Minnes in the middle of all his mirth that I never saw any man so out-done in all my life; and Sir J. Minnes's mirth to see himself out-done was the crown of all our mirth.

And Gardiner adds, 'Isn't that a wonderful picture? And think of the grave John Evelyn having this gaiety in him!'.

A. G. Gardiner, *Leaves in the Wind*, 1920

Ah, London! London! our delight,
Great flower that opens but at night,
Great City of the Midnight Sun,
Whose day begins when day is done.

Lamp after lamp against the sky
Open a sudden beaming eye,
Leaping alight on either hand
The iron lilies of the Strand.

Like dragon flies, the hansoms hover,
With jewelled eyes, to catch the lover;
The streets are full of lights and loves,
Soft gowns, and flutter of nocturnal doves.

The human moths about the light
Dash and cling close in dazed delight,
And burn and laugh, the world and wife,
For this is London, this is life!

Richard Le Gallienne, from 'A Ballad of London'

Our part of London, like Kensington or Islington, is
but the formless accretion of countless swarms of life
which had no common endeavour; and so here we are,
Time's latest deposit, the vascular stratum of this area
of the earth's rind, a sensitive surface flourishing
during its day on the piled strata of the dead. Yet this
is the reef to which I am connected by tissue and
bone. Cut the kind of life you find in Poplar, and I
must bleed. I cannot detach myself, and write of it.
Like any other atom, I would show the local dirt,
if examined. My hand moves, not loyally so much as
instinctively, to impulses which come from beneath
and so out of a stranger's knowledge; out of my own,
too, largely.

H. M. Tomlinson, *London River*, 1921

*Vittorio de Vincenti was an Italian dancer who
appeared in London at the Alhambra in 1890 and 1892.
He clearly impressed Shaw, who elsewhere described
his as 'the best male dancer I have ever seen'.*

When I arrived at my door after these dissipations I
found Fitzroy Square, in which I live, deserted. It was
a clear, dry, cold night; and the carriageway round
the circular railing presented such a magnificent hippo-
drome that I could not resist trying to go just once
round in Vincenti's fashion. It proved frightfully
difficult. After my fourteenth fall I was picked up by
a policeman. 'What are you doing here?', he said,
keeping fast hold of me. 'I bin watching you for the
last five minutes.' I explained, eloquently and enthusiastically. He hesitated a moment, and then said, 'Would
you mind holding my helmet while I have a try? It
don't look so hard.' Next moment his nose was buried
in the macadam and his right knee was out through
its torn garment. He got up bruised and bleeding, but
resolute. 'I never was beaten yet,' he said; 'and I won't
be beaten now. It was my coat that tripped me.' We
both hung our coats on the railings, and went at it
again. If each round of the square had been a round

in a prize fight, we should have been less damaged
and disfigured; but we persevered, and by four o'clock
the policeman had just succeeded in getting round
twice without a rest or a fall, when an inspector arrived
and asked him bitterly whether that was his notion
of fixed point duty. 'I allow it ain't fixed point,' said
the constable, emboldened by his new accomplishment,
'but I'll lay half a sovereign *you* can't do it.' The
inspector could not resist the temptation to try (I was
whirling round before his eyes in the most fascinating
manner); and he made rapid progress after half an hour
or so. We were subsequently joined by an early postman and by a milkman, who unfortunately broke his
leg and had to be carried to hospital by the other
three. By that time I was quite exhausted, and could
hardly crawl into bed. It was perhaps a foolish scene,
but nobody who has witnessed Vincenti's performance
will be surprised at it.

G. B. Shaw, *The Star*, 21 February 1890

'Anything about Ireland always makes me cry', said
the fat woman. 'I don't know why; I come from
Peckham.'

W. Pett Ridge, *London Only*

It was these ardent good intentions, this burning social conscience, as well as the desire to do the emancipated thing, that drove Stanley, leaving Oxford in 1882, to take up settlement work in Poplar. So Poplarised, so orientalised, did she become, that she took to speaking of her parental home in Bloomsbury as being in the West End. To her, everything west of St Paul's became the West End. The West End, its locality and its limits, is indeed a debatable land. Where you think it is seems to depend on where you live or work. To those who work in Fleet Street, as do so many journalists, it seems that anything west of the Strand is the West End. 'West End Cocaine Orgy', you see on newspaper placards, and find that the orgy occurred in Piccadilly or Soho. Mayfair and its environs are also spoken of by these scribblers of the east as the West End. But to those who live in Mayfair, the West End begins at about Edgware Road, and Mayfair seems about the middle, and to the denizens of Edgware Road the West End is Bayswater, Kensington, or Shepherd's Bush. The dwellers in these outlying lands of the sunset do really acknowledge that they are the West End; and to them Mayfair and Piccadilly are not even the middle, but the east. A strange, irrational phrase, which bears so fluctuating and dubious a meaning. But then nearly all phrases are strange and irrational, like most of those who use them.

Rose Macaulay, *Told By an Idiot*, 1923

Hearts just as pure and fair
May beat in Belgrave Square
As in the lowly air
of Seven Dials.

W. S. Gilbert, *Iolanthe*, 1882

Transports of Delight

A city so diffuse sets problems of mobility which
become awe-inspiring. Next to the weather, transport
has been the most widely popular theme of small talk.
Exiled Londoners, asked to express their wretchedness,
have seen the loss of their birthright in the symbol of
the London bus. Or perhaps in the racketing of the
underground train. Or in the succession of broughams,
growlers, hansoms, taxis, which have conveyed Our
Betters to their assignations over the centuries.

Picture a disused platform of a rather forgotten station,
let us say South Hampstead, the first station after
Euston on the old LMS electric line to Watford. It
opens late and shuts early and few people seem to use
it. When I was a boy we called it Loudon Road and
the booking office building stood, as it still stands,
looking rather like a small mid-Victorian brick Vicarage,
harmonising happily with the Gothic fancies of this
lilac-shaded part of St John's Wood. I should think
from the style of architecture it was built in the late
'seventies by which time enough platforms had been
constructed at Euston to make it possible for the
London and North-Western to run an enlarged suburban service. I have never departed from nor alighted
at South Hampstead. Not being modern, my hours are
too long either side of the day to take advantage of its
times of opening. I prefer to imagine the station. I
like to think that it contains the various fittings of a
former age for which my eye is always on the watch
when I use an unfamiliar station. Perhaps there are
some very old tickets in the booking office – a first-class

[46]

return to Chalk Farm (which would mean going down to Euston and coming back again), would probably be printed with 'Loudon Road' and the letters LNWR. Under the treads of the stairs to the platform there may be those tin advertisements saying IRON JELLOIDS, IRON JELLOIDS, IRON JELLOIDS in blue on an orange ground, insisting as one ascends, on the weakness of one's heart and its need for the stamina which those pills supply. Still in imagination, I walk right down to the end of the platform to the oldest lamp standard, a graceful thing on twisted columns with, perhaps, a six-sided glass cage for the gas-burner and the name of the iron foundry where it was made at the base of its column. Against the station wall there may be tin signs for MAZAWATTEE TEA and the still-familiar black and blue splodge of STEPHEN'S INK on a white ground. And, of course, there will be those two old friends VENO'S LIGHTNING COUGH CURE and DR. J. COLLIS BROWNE'S CHLORODYNE.

Then what waiting rooms there may not be! Gothic Revival cast-iron grates in which no fire has been lighted since the days when a mountain of glowing coal warmed the early morning pin-striped bottoms of city gentlemen who used this station as the preliminary part of a journey from Boundary Road to Euston, thence by steam train on the inner circle from Euston Square to Aldersgate. (Ah, Aldersgate! alas the Refreshment Room has been bombed, the Refreshment Room at the top of the steps surveying all four platforms from the height of the great semi-circular glass roof, that Refreshment Room where, as Mr John Hayward once pointed out to me, the words AFTERNOON TEAS A SPECIALITY were affixed in letters of white china to the plate-glass window). The walls of the waiting room will be green. The lighting gas. There will perhaps be a framed collection of photographs, 'Beauty spots of the L and NWR; Killarney; Sackville Street, Dublin; Blarney Castle (the L and NW always liked to give the impression that it owned all the Irish railways); George's Landing Stage, Liverpool; Bettws-y-coed; Warwick Castle'. These will be in sepia with gilt lettering on the wooden surround. Then there will be a framed looking-glass in which it will be impossible to see all one's face at once because painted on the surface are the words IDRIS TABLE WATERS and a long maiden in clothes rather like a water lily holding in her hand a sparkling glass of IDRIS. These are but some of the delights I imagine there may be at South Hampstead.

John Betjeman, *First and Last Loves*, 1952

I had a very elderly and esteemed relative who once told me that while walking along the Strand he met a lion that had escaped from Exeter Change menagerie. I said, 'What did you do?', and he looked at me with contempt as if the question were imbecile. 'DO?', he said, 'Why, I took a cab.'

Ford Madox Ford, *Ancient Lights*, 1911

The railway termini on the north side of London have been kept as remote as Eastry had kept the railway station from Wimblehurst, they stop on the very outskirts of the estates, but from the south, the South Eastern railway had butted its great, stupid, rusty iron head of Charing Cross Station – that great head that came smashing down in 1905 – clean across the river, between Somerset House and Whitehall. The south side had no protecting estates. Factory chimneys smoke right over against Westminster with an air of carelessly not having permission, and the whole effect of industrial London and of all London east of Temple Bar and of the huge, dingy immensity of London port, is to me of something disproportionately large, something morbidly expanded, without plan or intention, dark and sinister toward the clean, clear social assurance of the West End. And south of this central London, south-east, south-west, far west, north-west, all round the northern hills, are similar disproportionate growths, endless streets of undistinguished houses, undistinguished industries, shabby families, second-rate shops, inexplicable people who in a once fashionable phrase do not 'exist'. All these aspects have suggested to my mind at times, do suggest to this day, the unorganised, abundant substance of some tumorous growth-process, a process which indeed bursts all the outlines of the affected carcass and protrudes such masses as ignoble, comfortable Croydon, as tragic, impoverished East Ham. To this day I ask myself will those masses ever become structural, will they indeed shape into anything new whatever, or is that cancerous image their true and ultimate diagnosis?

H. G. Wells, *Tono-Bungay*, 1909

My daily walks to and from Spreckley's in Cannon Street were always during the rush hour, and the traffic congestion was usually worse than anything the impatient Londoner has put up with at any time since then – especially, and to me inexplicably, on a wet Friday. Motor vehicles were becoming commonplace. Unless they were in some way eccentric, like Mr Solly Joel's famous and noiseless electric brougham or some such exciting foreign automobile as the Isott-Fraccini, the Darracq, or the Hispano-Suiza, they no longer turned many heads. They were all subject to a maximum speed limit of twenty miles an hour, and in some districts (though not in the City) there were local limits as low as five. Motor buses were limited to twelve, but in the City they had little chance to attain even that. At this time they were 'Old Bill' buses, the model famous for its use in France by the

Army Service Corps as troop transport. These seemed to me at the time, and still seem, about the ugliest vehicles ever designed since the advent of the wheel. They were greatly mistrusted by some of the road safety authorities; and by way of example I recently found in the Minutes of the Fulham Borough Council for 1 November 1911 a complaint about motor omnibuses and their 'damage to roadways, vibration, serious annoyance to inhabitants, positive danger to premises along the route, and loss of rates from premises vacated by victims'. Motor buses had first appeared in London in 1905, and their drivers were often prosecuted for dangerous driving by racing – 'Vanguards' (petrol driven) versus 'metropolitan' (steam) buses. The Old Bill b' ses were fitted with a so-called lifeguard between front and rear wheels on each side, an arrangement of wooden slats angled so as to deflect outwards, and clear of the back wheels, anyone falling against the side of the bus. I never understood what it did to anyone run over by a front wheel, but preferred not to think of that.

Except along the broad Victoria Embankment, where they were confined to the river side of the roadway, tramcars had never been allowed in the City of London. The rails carrying these wonderful and lamented vehicles came to an abrupt end at various points round the City boundary – Gray's Inn Road, Hatton Garden, Faringdon Street, Bishopsgate, and Southwark Bridge.

Horse-drawn vehicles abounded everywhere, mixed in-
congruously with the growing throng of motor buses,
taxi cabs and lorries. As I walked through narrow
thoroughfares like Carter Lane, Knightrider Street and
Bread Street I was always astounded at the skill of the
carmen navigating heavy pair-horsed wagons in those
confined spaces: they had the advantage that they
could turn in their own length, the front wheels turning
right in beneath the undercarriage. The stumbling
horses seemed always to help intelligently and willingly
in the process, and almost able to do it unaided; there
was little use of the whip and not much shouting.
Falled horses, were, however, a frequent sight. And
once down, they were seldom able to get up while still
in the shafts, and there was a general traffic hold-up
while they were released from the harness, scrambled
up with a clatter of iron shoes, and stood waiting
patiently to be re-harnessed. I believe there was much
cruelty to horses in those days, on the part of owners
and carmen in whom the only emotions kindled by a
horse were anger and impatience. And there were City
policemen, usually ex-cavalrymen, who were horsey ex-
perts as well as born prosecutors, and who spent most
of their time at the magistrates' courts waiting for some
cruelty case to be called on, while the ill-treated horse
waited in the yard outside, with protruding haunch-
bones or one hoof held limply.

C. H. Rolph, *London Particulars*, 1980

You may not realise that when the tubes cease work
the current is switched off in sections. As each section
becomes juiceless, gangs of men waiting at the stations
set out to examine every yard of the 171 miles of track
on the Tube and District systems. It is probably the
most important four hours work during the London
night. Every nut, bolt, screw, lamp, wire, signal, tele-
phone, disc, sleeper, key and rail is hit and prodded
and peered at; they even go over every yard of the
great iron ribs of the tunnels. They wander on like

explorers in an Egyptian tomb – and this resemblance is intensified by occasional mosquitoes which live in the even temperature all the year long. I did not see one. I am told, however, that gangers who go to sleep often awaken bitten; but as a stray ganger is the only brightness in the life of a Tube mosquito – for they never penetrate to the richer potentialities of the stations – who shall grudge them an infrequent happiness?

H. V. Morton, *The Heart of London*, 1925

Breakfast over, the whole family walked in detachments to St Paul's Cathedral. We had reduced the route to a science, by side streets, short cuts by the New River, along parts of Essex Road, the City Road, Goswell Road, and Aldersgate, and finally past the 'highest point of London' in Panyer Alley to the north door of the cathedral. I must have been very little when I did this long walk, because I once described it as 'continually cwossing'. My father explained to me that the more slantingly you crossed a road the shorter it was. He also alleviated the walk by playing wayside cribbage, a favourite game in the country. In town the points for scoring had to be rather different; thus we had: man carrying baby, 5; three in a hansom, 5; perambulator, 1; cat in a window, 15; ladder, 1; man with a mourning hatband, 5; anyone we knew to speak to (very rare) 31, game. I think we must have played this when mother was walking behind, or this game would never have slipped through her rules.

Sometimes mother and I went by tram, but the horse affair was so slow, the waiting for it so long, and the stoppings so frequent, that the walkers reached Aldersgate before we did. Occasionally my father would vary the route home by taking us through the deserted City, free of all traffic, and showing us Austin Friars and funny little passages, till we came to Broad Street and thence back to Canonbury by train.

Molly Hughes, *A London Child of the Seventies*, 1934

Friday January 27, 1899.

A few nights ago – we had been to the Empire, Sharpe, Mater, Sep and I – there was a gale. In the usual midnight altercation at Piccadilly Circus for the inside seats of omnibuses we had suffered defeat; we sat on the inclement top of the vehicle, a disconsolate row of four, cowering behind the waterproof aprons (which were not waterproof), and exchanging fragments of pessimistic philosophy.

We knew we were taking cold; at first we were annoyed, but with increasing numbness came resignation. We grew calm enough to take an interest in the imperturbable driver, who nonchalantly and with perfect technique steered his dogged horses through the tortuous mazes of traffic, never speaking, never stirring, only answering like an automaton to the conductor's bell. Some drivers will gossip, but this one had apparently his own preoccupations. We could see only his hat, some grey hairs, his rotund cape, and his enormous gloved hands, and perhaps we began to wonder what sort of man he was. For mile after mile he drove forward in a Trappist silence till we were verging on Putney, and the rain-washed thoroughfares reflected only the gaslights and the forbidding façades of the houses. Then at last, but without moving his head, he suddenly joined the conversation.

'I've been out in worse', he said. 'Yes, we gets used to it. But we gets so we HAS to live out of doors. If I got a indoor job I should die. I have to go out for a walk afore I can eat my breakfast.'

A pause, and then:

'I've driven these roads for eight and twenty year, and the only pal I've found is Cod Liver Oil. From September to March I takes it, and I never has rheumatism and I never has colds nor nothing o' that sort. I give it my children ever since they was born, and now I'm blessed if they don't cry for it.'

He finished; but he had imparted his wisdom, delivered his message, and with the fine instinct denied to so many literary artists, he knew when to be silent. We asked him to stop, and he did so without a word. 'Good night', we said; but he had done with speech for that evening, and gave us no reply. We alighted. The bus rolled away into the mirror-like vista of the street.

The Journals of Arnold Bennett 1896–1928

February 10, Sunday

Contrary to my wishes, Carrie allowed Lupin to persuade her to take her for a drive in the afternoon in his trap. I quite disapprove of driving on a Sunday, but I did not like to trust Carrie alone with Lupin, so I offered to go too. Lupin said: 'Now, that is nice of you, Guv; but you won't mind sitting on the back-seat of the cart?'

Lupin proceeded to put on a bright-blue coat that seemed miles too large for him. Carrie said it wanted taking in considerably at the back. Lupin said; 'Haven't you seen a box-coat before? You can't drive in anything else.'

He may wear what he likes in the future, for I shall never drive with him again. His conduct was shocking. When we passed Highgate Archway, he tried to pass everything and everybody. He shouted to respectable people who were walking quietly in the road to get out of the way; he flicked at the horse of an old man who was riding, causing it to rear; and, as I had to ride backwards, I was compelled to face a gang of roughs in a donkey-cart whom Lupin had chaffed, and who turned and followed us for nearly a mile, bellowing, indulging in coarse jokes and laughter, to say nothing of occasionally pelting us with orange-peel.

Lupin's excuse – that the Prince of Wales would have to put up with the same sort of thing if he drove to the Derby – was of little consolation to either Carrie or myself.

G. and W. Grossmith, *The Diary of a Nobody*, 1892

My uncle Sydney, Grump's only son, used to tell a story of Christmastide, when Grumps, after collecting much provender for the family, meeting many friends in London, and with difficulty catching the last train from King's Cross to Wood Green, sprang into the guard's van at the rear of this train, a goose and other matters sprawling from his arms upon the floor. As he looked about the van to exchange cordial and self-congratulatory greetings with the guard, he saw that no guard was there. Instantly he realised that the guard must have been left behind, stranded upon Christmas Eve; and since in his case action was as rapid as thought, he leapt to the brakes, applied them, and brought the labouring train to stand. He then waited for the grateful thanks of the missing man but, instead, a crazy shouting assailed his ears. He leaned comfortably from the window of the guard's van, smiling at the occurrence of this curious incident upon Christmas Eve, and peering back towards King's Cross for the dilatory guard. There were lights upon the line; he saw men running. It then appeared that the guard had all the time been safely settled in another van at the front of the train, and that promptitude had allowed time for but an imperfect survey of the possibilities. So far from receiving gratitude, Grumps travelled the rest of the way to Wood Green in disgrace.

When he arrived there, it was raining rather hard, no cab was available, and he had to climb what seemed to him to be an almost ridiculously steep hill called the Jolly Butchers, up which he could not struggle with the ever-increasing weight of good things which formed his burden. But, always full of resource, he divided his parcels into two equal lots. With one of them he trudged through the rain for a certain distance then he set down the first load, ran back for the other, which he took a stage farther; and so, in the pouring darkness of the early morning, with Winter about him, down his neck, and into his boots, he succeeded in reaching home with all packages, the goose, and some precious bottles intact: his heart sober and triumphant; the top hat which he always wore still borne, however sodden, with dignity upon his weary head.

Frank Swinnerton, *Autobiography*, 1937

One day stands out vividly in my memory. I think I must have been about nine years of age. We took the train to Ludgate Hill, and a railway journey always gave me much pleasure. The train passed through green fields until it reached our station; from then onwards it was all bricks and mortar. We passed through some of the poorest industrial districts and wormed our way between shabby factories, blocks of dreary dwellings, and all the incomprehensible muddle of the slums. Over bridges spanning busy shopping centres, into grimy stations that seemed to be held together by tin advertisement signs, through the smoke-begrimed Elephant and Castle and Borough Road, and then out on to the iron cage that spans the Thames, with Blackfriars Bridge on the left, bursting with horse traffic, and St Paul's great dome looming on the right like a sepia cloud, for here was an overhead fog, a canopy of saffron, with the deep red sun throwing a wonderful light on mighty, smoky warehouses and giving them an uncertain beauty. The train threaded its way into the dark causeways between them into the very heart of the City of London. Uncle James and family were waiting for us in the bookhall of Ludgate Hill station. What a joyous meeting! All of us got up to kill, and giving the impression of people enjoying an income five times the extent of our real one.

Frederick Willis, *A Book of London Yesterdays*, 1960

When the railway clerk asked me what place I wanted tickets for, London sprang to my mouth promptly in a murmur, and taking the tickets, I replied to Temple,—

'The rest of the way by rail. Uberly's sure to stop at that inn.'...

Later we were in yellow fog, then in brown. Temple

stared at both windows and at me; he jumped from
his seat and fell on it, muttering, 'No; nonsense! I say!'
but he had accurately recognised London's fog. I left
him unanswered to bring up all his senses, which the
railway had outstripped, for the contemplation of this
fact, that we two were in the city of London.

. . .

It was London city, and the Bench was the kernel
of it to me. I throbbed with excitement, though I sat
looking out of the windows into the subterranean
atmosphere quite still and firm. When you think long
undividedly of a single object it gathers light, and
when you draw near it in person the strange thing to
your mind is the absence of that light; but I, approaching it in this dense fog, seemed to myself to be only
thinking of it a little more warmly than usual, and
instead of fading it reversed the process, and became,
from light, luminous. Not being able, however, to
imagine the Bench a happy place, I corrected the excess
of brightness and gave its walls a pine-torch glow; I
set them in the middle of a great square, and hung the
standard of England drooping over them in a sort of
mournful family pride. Then, because I next conceived
it a foreign kind of place, different altogether from that
home growth of ours, the Tower of London, I topped
it with a multitude of domes of pumpkin or turban
shape, resembling the Kremlin of Moscow, which had
once leapt up in the eye of winter, glowing like a
million pine-torches, and flung shadows of stretching
red horses on the black smoke-drift. But what was the
Kremlin, that had seen a city perish, to this Bench
where my father languished! There was no comparing
them for tragic horror. And the Kremlin had snow-
fields around it; this Bench was caught out of sight,
hemmed in by an atmosphere thick as Charon breathed;
it might as well be underground.

'Oh! it's London,' Temple went on, correcting his
incorrigible doubts about it. He jumped on the platform; we had to call out not to lose one another. 'I

say, Richie, this is London,' he said, linking his arm in mine: 'you know by the size of the station; and besides, there's the fog. Oh! it's London. We've over-shot it, we're positively in London.'

I could spare no sympathy for his feelings, and I did not respond to his inquiring looks. Now that we were here I certainly wished myself away, though I would not have retreated, and for awhile I was glad of the discomforts besetting me; my step was hearty as I led on, meditating upon asking some one the direction to the Bench presently. We had to walk, and it was nothing but traversing on a slippery pave-ment atmospheric circles of black brown and brown red, and sometimes a larger circle of pale yellow; the colours of old bruised fruits, medlars, melons, and the smell of them; nothing is more desolate. Neither of us knew where we were, nor where we were going. We struggled through an interminable succession of squalid streets, from the one lamp visible to its neighbour in the darkness: you might have fancied yourself peering at the head of an old saint on a smoky canvas; it was like the painting of light rather than light. Figures rushed by; we saw no faces.

Temple spoke solemnly: 'Our dinner-hour at home is half-past six.'

A street-boy overheard him and chaffed him. Temple got the worst of it, and it did him good, for he had the sweetest nature in the world. We declined to be attended by link-boys; they would have hurt our sense of independence. Possessed of a sovereign faith that, by dint of resolution, I should ultimately penetrate to the great square enclosing the Bench, I walked with the air of one who had the map of London in his eye and could thread it blindfold. Temple was thereby deceived into thinking that I must somehow have learnt the direction I meant to take, and knew my way, though at the slightest indication of my halting and glancing round his suspicions began to boil, and he was for asking some one the name of the ground we

Chapel and Gateway, Lincoln's Inn

stood on: he murmured, 'Fellows get lost in London.'
By this time he clearly understood that I had come to
London on purpose; he could not but be aware of the
object of my coming, and I was too proud, and he still
too delicate, to allude to it.

The fog choked us. Perhaps it took away the sense
of hunger by filling us as if we had eaten a dinner
of soot. We had no craving to eat until long past
the dinner-hour in Temple's house, and then I would
rather have plunged into a bath and a bed than have
been requested to sit at a feast; Temple, too, I fancy.

George Meredith, *The Adventures of Harry
Richmond*, 1870

On the construction of St Pancras.

It was decided to bridge the canal. In order to do this
the very large and very crowded burial ground of old
St Pancras would have to be levelled. When the work
started, skulls and bones were seen lying about; a
passer-by saw an open coffin staved in through which
peeped a bright tress of hair. Great scandal was caused
and the company was forced to arrange for a reverent

reburial. The architect in charge of this reburial was A. W. Blomfield, and he sent one of his assistants to watch the carrying away of the dead to see that it was reverently done. That assistant was Thomas Hardy, and his poems 'The Levelled Churchyard' and 'In the Cemetery' recall the fact. Once when he and Blomfield met on the site they found a coffin which contained two skulls:

> O Passenger, pray list and catch
> Our sighs and piteous groans,
> Half stifled in this jumbled patch
> Of wrenched memorial stones.
>
> We late-lamented, resting here,
> Are mixed to human jam,
> And each to each exclaims in fear,
> 'I know not which I am!'

John Betjeman, *London's Historic Railway Stations*,
1972

There is one station which hardly anyone uses at all, Broad Street, which is given over to ghosts of frock-coated citizens who once crowded the old North London trains from the steam suburbs of Highbury, Canonbury and Camden Town. Often do those sumptuous LMS electric trains swing across the north London suburbs on that smooth, useless, beautiful journey to Richmond. At no time of day have I known it impossible to find a seat in their spacious carriages. And the frock-coated ones are dead and gone like the rolling stock which carried them, their houses have been turned into flats, their gardens built over by factories. The North London was the last line to use wooden-seated third-class carriages as it did on its Poplar branch (now closed), the last line in London to run no trains during church time on a Sunday morning, and within living memory the General Manager of the line refused to allow Smith's bookstall on Broad Street to sell any vulgar-looking papers. Still the trains run, through haunted gas-lit stations, on the most revealing train journey London can provide.

John Betjeman, *First and Last Loves*, 1952

We would go into the High Street and go up and down in Derry and Tom's lifts, up in one and down in another, till the lift attendants grew tired of us, which before long they did. After that we would go into High Street Kensington station and buy 1½d. tickets to the next station, and get into the sooty train and travel all round the Inner Circle, which took about an hour, and when we got out at High Street again we were black with soot and choking like chimney sweeps, but we felt we had had a fine lot of travelling for three halfpence and had swindled the Railway Company. One day we went to Baker Street, and looked for number 221A because of Holmes and Watson, but we could not find it, so we walked along Baker Street tracking criminals and noting where they went, and more than once we thought we saw Watson, who was more frequent then than now, but we never saw Holmes with his deerstalker and ulster and cocaine, searching the pavement for clues.

Rose Macaulay, *Coming to London*, 1957

'Why, bless my soul, in the good old days we had to have a regular baby hunt nearly every night under the seats of the old trains. Anybody who didn't want a baby seemed to leave it in the Underground.'

H. V. Morton, *The Heart of London*, 1925

The Roots of Fiction

No city has ever stimulated the reveries of story-telling
more prolifically. The more we read of the private
lives of the story-tellers, the clearer become the images
of actuality which inspired the tales. It used to be the
fashion for literary theorists to deride writers like
Dickens and Wilkie Collins as purveyors of crude
melodrama, it evidently never becoming apparent to
them that there existed other literary sources which
explained, for instance, the creation of those two
notorious women in white, Miss Havisham and Laura
Fairlie. Dickens himself metamorphosed into one of his
own characters, while lesser novelists borrowed London's
topographical effects for their stories.

Another very different person who stopped our growth,
we associate with Berners Street, Oxford Street;
whether she was constantly on parade in that street
only, or was ever to be seen elsewhere, we are unable to
say. The White Woman is her name. She is dressed
entirely in white, with a ghastly white plating round
her head and face, inside her white bonnet. She even
carries (we hope) a white umbrella. With white boots,
we know she picks her way through the winter dirt.
She is a conceited old creature, cold and formal in
manner, and evidently went simpering mad on personal
grounds alone – no doubt because a wealthy Quaker
wouldn't marry her. This is her bridal dress. She is
always walking up here, on her way to church to
marry the false Quaker. We observe in her mincing
step and fishy eye that she intends to lead him a hard

life. We stopped growing when we got at the conclusion that the Quaker had had a happy escape of the White Woman.

Charles Dickens, *Household Words*: 'When We Stopped Growing', 1853

An inquest was held on the 29th, on Martha Joachim, a Wealthy and Eccentric Lady, late of 27, York Buildings, Marylebone, aged 62. The jury proceeded to view the body, but had to beat a sudden retreat, until a bulldog, belonging to deceased, and which savagely attacked them, was secured. It was shown in evidence that on June 1st, 1808, her father, an officer in the Life Guards, was murdered and robbed in the Regent's Park. A reward of £300 was offered for the murderer, who was apprehended with the property upon him, and executed. In 1825, a suitor of the deceased, whom her mother rejected, shot himself while sitting on the sofa with her, and she was covered with his brains. From that instant she lost her reason. Since her mother's death, eighteen years ago, she had led the life of a recluse, dressed in white, and never going out. A charwoman occasionally brought her what supplied her wants. Her only companions were the bulldog, which she nursed like a child, and two cats. Her house was filled with images of soldiers in lead, which she called her 'body-guards'. When the collectors called for their taxes, they had to cross the garden-wall to gain admission. One morning she was found dead in her bed; and a surgeon who was called in, said she had died of bronchitis and might have recovered with proper medical aid. The jury returned a verdict to that effect.

From *Household Words*, edited by Charles Dickens, January 1850

One night in the '50's Millais was returning home to 83, Gower Street from one of the many parties held under Mrs Collins's hospitable roof in Hanover Terrace, and, in accordance with the usual practice of the two brothers, Wilkie and Charles, they accompanied him on his homeward walk through the dimly-lit, and in those days semi-rural roads and lanes of North London ... It was a beautiful moonlight night in the summer time and as the three friends walked along chatting gaily together, they were suddenly arrested by a piercing scream coming from the garden of a villa close at hand. It was evidently the cry of a woman in distress; and while pausing to consider what they should do, the iron gate leading to the garden was dashed open, and from it came the figure of a very young and very beautiful woman dressed in flowing white robes that shone in the moonlight. She seemed to float rather than run in their direction, and on coming up to the three young men, she paused for a moment in an attitude of supplication and terror. Then, suddenly seeming to recollect herself, she suddenly moved on and vanished in the shadows cast upon the road.

'What a lovely woman!', was all Millais could say. 'I must see who she is, and what is the matter', said Wilkie Collins, as, without a word he dashed off after her. His two companions waited in vain for his return, and next day, when they met again, he seemed indisposed to talk of his adventure. They gathered from him, however, that he had come up with the lovely fugitive and had heard from her own lips the history of her life and the cause of her sudden flight. She was a young lady of good birth and position, who had accidentally fallen into the hands of a man living in a villa in Regent's Park. There for many months he kept her prisoner under threats and mesmeric influence of so alarming a character that she dared not attempt to escape, until, in sheer desperation, she fled from the brute, who, with a poker in his hand, threatened to dash her brains out. Her subsequent history, interesting as it is, is not for these pages.

J. G. Millais, *The Life of John Everett Millais*, 1899

George Sala spies Dickens:

A hansom cab whirled you by the Bell and Horns at Brompton, and there he was striding, as with seven-league boots, seemingly in the direction of North-end, Fulham. The Metropolitan Railway set you forth at Lisson Grove, and you met him plodding speedily towards the Yorkshire Stingo. He was to be met rapidly skirting the grim black wall of the prison in Coldbath Fields, or trudging along the Seven Sisters road at Holloway, or bearing, under a steady press of sail, underneath Highgate Archway, or pursuing the even tenor of his way up the Vauxhall Bridge Road.

George Sala (1828–96)

A stone's-throw from the Strand, London's best-known street, the Adelphi precinct had a curious privacy of its own. It led to nowhere. Its tenants in its last fifty years were early-closing learned societies and businesses and late-closing Bohemian clubs, a faded Dickensian hotel, some old-fashioned residents, mainly actors, and romantic tenants whose wardrobe was said to consist of evening clothes and pyjamas. In front where the river used to run were the Embankment Gardens, closed at night. Save on the big nights at the old Savage Club, when the West End came to Bohemia, it had a forgotten and derelict look, especially when the two great hotels to the east of it, the Cecil and the Savoy, were blazing with lights. Stevenson clearly chose it for the setting of his Box Court and the Suicide Club...

James Bone, *London Echoing*, 1948

He walked from Norfolk Street into the Strand, and there the world was still alive, though it was now nearly one o'clock. The debauched misery, the wretched outdoor midnight revelry of the world was there, streaming in and out from gin-palaces, and bawling itself hoarse with horrid, discordant screech-owl slang. But he went his way unheeding and uncontaminated. Now, now that it was useless, he was thinking of the better things of the world; nothing now seemed worth his grasp, nothing now seemed pleasurable, nothing capable of giving joy, but what was decent, good, reputable, cleanly, and polished. How he hated now that lower world with which he had for the last three years condescended to pass so much of his time! how he hated himself for his own vileness! He thought of what Alaric was, of what Norman was, of what he himself might have been – he that was praised by Mrs Woodward for his talent, he that was encouraged to place himself among the authors of the day! He thought of all this, and then he thought of what he was – the affianced husband of Norah Geraghy!

He went along the Strand, over the crossing under the statue of Charles on horseback, and up Pall Mall East till he came to the opening into the park under the Duke of York's column. The London night world was all alive as he made his way. From the Opera Colonnade shrill shrieked out at him as he passed, and drunken men coming down from the night supper-houses in the Haymarket saluted him with affectionate cordiality. The hoarse waterman from the cabstand, whose voice had perished in the night air, croaked out at him the offer of a vehicle; and one of the night beggar-women who cling like burrs to those who roam

Haymarket Theatre

the street at these unhallowed hours stuck to him, as
she had done ever since he entered the Strand . . . His
way home would have taken him up Waterloo Place,
but the space round the column was now deserted and
quiet, and sauntering there, without thinking of what
he did, he paced up and down between the Clubs and
the steps leading into the park. There, walking to and
fro slowly, he thought of his past career, of all the
circumstances of his life since his life had been left to
his own control, and of the absence of all hope for
the future.

Anthony Trollope, *The Three Clerks*, 1858

*Between 1879 and 1883, the unknown Irishman George
Bernard Shaw composed five 'novels of my nonage'
which were so far in advance of their time as to be
utterly unsaleable. At last Shaw buried the novelist in
him forever and turned his attention to polemics,
journalism, and at last the stage. For the rest of his
life he persisted in referring derisively to the novels as
his five brown paper parcels, which belatedly proved
themselves to be delightfully readable. During the
period of their composition, Shaw moved from Victoria
Grove, Fulham, to the area where the Euston and
Marylebone Roads merge into each other, living with
his mother first in Fitzroy Street and then in Osnaburgh
Street. At least one moment in one of the five brown
paper parcels sounds less like fiction than reminiscence:*

As the door closed on her, he turned towards Fitzroy
Square; but a feeling of being ill and out of conceit
with himself made him turn back to a restaurant in
Oxford Street, where he had a chop and a glass of
wine. After this, his ardour suddenly revived; and he
hurried towards Aurelie's residence by way of Wells
Street. He soon lost his way in the labyrinth between
Great Portland and Cleveland Streets, and at last
emerged at Portland Road railway station. Knowing the
way thence, he started afresh for Fitzroy Square.

Before he had gone many steps he was arrested by his mother's voice calling him. She was coming from the station, and overtook him in the Euston Road, at the corner of Southampton Street.

'What on earth are you doing in this quarter of the town?', he said, stopping, and trying to conceal how unwelcome the interruption was.

'That is a question which you have no right to ask, Adrian. People who have "Where are you going," and "What are you doing" always in their mouths are social and domestic nuisances, as I have often told you. However, I am going to buy some curtains in Tottenham Court Road.'

Bernard Shaw, *Love Among the Artists*, 1883

The View from Outside

What do they know of London who only London know? The Irish, the Canadians, the French, the Russians and the Americans among others have left their impressions of the city they came to examine. Some refused to take it seriously, while others, especially Henry James, took it much too seriously, arming themselves against social disgrace even in the face of a purely conjectural death.

The city is able to boast of many handsome public buildings and offices which compare favourably with anything on the other side of the Atlantic. On the bank of the Thames itself rises the power house of the Westminster Electric Supply Corporation, a handsome modern edifice in the later Japanese style. Close by are the commodious premises of the Imperial Tobacco Company, while at no great distance the Chelsea Gas Works add a striking feature of rotundity. Passing northward, one observes Westminster Bridge, notably as a principal station of the Underground Railway. This station and the one next above it, the Charing Cross one, are connected by a wide thoroughfare called Whitehall. One of the best American drug stores is here situated. The upper end of Whitehall opens into the majestic and spacious Trafalgar Square. Here are grouped in imposing proximity the offices of the Canadian Pacific and other railways, the International Sleeping Car Company, the Montreal 'Star', and the Anglo-Dutch bank. Two of the best American barber shops are conveniently grouped near the square, while the existence of a tall stone monument in the middle of the Square itself enables the American visitor to find them without difficulty. Passing eastward towards the heart of the City, one notes on the left hand the imposing pile of St Paul's, an enormous church with a round dome at the top, suggesting strongly the first Church of Christ (Scientist) on Euclid Avenue, Cleveland. But, the English churches not being labelled, the visitor is often at a loss to distinguish them.

A little further on one finds oneself in the heart of financial London. Here are all the great financial institutions of America – The First National Bank of Milwaukee, the Planters' National Bank of St Louis, The Montana Farmers Trust Co, and many others – have either their offices or their agents. The Bank of England, which acts as the London agent of the Montana Farmers Trust Company, and the London County Bank, which represents the People's Deposit Co. of Yonkers, N.Y., are said to be in the neighbourhood.

This particular part of London is connected with the existence of that strange and mysterious thing called 'the City'. I am still unable to decide whether the City is a person, or a place, or a thing. But as a form of being I give it credit for being the most emotional, the most volatile, the most peculiar creature in the world. You read in the morning paper that the City is 'deeply depressed'. At noon it is reported that the City is 'buoyant', and by four o'clock that the City is 'wildly excited'. I have tried in vain to find the causes of these peculiar changes of feeling. The ostensible reasons, as given in the newspaper, are so trivial as to be hardly worthy of belief. For example, here is the kind of news that comes out from the City: 'The news that a *modus vivendi* has been signed between the Sultan of Kowfat and the Shriek-ul-Islam has caused a sudden buoyancy in the City. Steel rails which had been depressed all morning reacted immediately, while American mules rose up sharply to par'...'Monsieur Poincaré, speaking at Bordeaux, said that henceforth

France must seek to retain by all possible means the
ping–pong championship of the world; values in the
City collapsed at once'...'Despatches from Bombay
say that the Shah of Persia yesterday handed a golden
slipper to the Grand Vizier Feebli Pasha as a sign that he
might go and chase himself. The news was at once
followed by a drop in oil, and a rapid attempt to
liquidate everything that is fluid.'

But these mysteries of the City I do not pretend to
explain. I have passed through the place dozens of
times and never noticed anything particular in the
way of depression or buoyancy, or falling oil, or rising
rails. But no doubt it is there.

Stephen Leacock, *My Discovery of England*, 1922

Staple Inn, Holborn

I went astray in Holborn through an arched entrance,
over which was 'Staple Inn'. In a court opening
inwards from this, there was a surrounding seclusion
of quiet dwelling houses, with beautiful green shrub-
bery and grass-plots in the court, and a great many
sunflowers in full bloom. The windows were open; it
was a lovely summer afternoon, and I have a sense
that bees were humming in the court, though this may
have been suggested by my fancy, because the sound
would have been so well suited to the scene. A boy

was reading at one of the windows. There was not a quieter spot in England than this, and it was very strange to have drifted into it so suddenly out of the bustle and rumble of Holborn; and to lose all this repose so suddenly, on passing through the arch of the outer court. In all the hundreds of years since London was built, it has not been able to sweep its roaring tide over that little island of quiet.

Nathaniel Hawthorne, *Passages from the English Notebooks*, 1870

People live with closed windows in August very much as they do in January, and there is to the eye no appreciable difference in the character – that is in the thickness and stiffness – of their coats and boots. A 'bath' in England, for the most part, all the year round, means a little portable tin tub and a sponge. Peaches and pears, grapes and melons, are not a more obvious ornament of the market at midsummer than at Christmas. This matter of peaches and melons, by the way, offers one of the best examples of that fact to which a commentator on English manners from afar finds himself constantly recurring, and to which he grows at last almost ashamed of alluding – the fact that the beauty and luxury of the country, that elaborate system known and revered all over the world as 'English comfort', is a limited and restricted, an essentially private, affair. I am not one of those irreverent strangers who talk of English fruit as a rather audacious *plaisanterie*, though I could see very well what was meant a short time since by an anecdote related to me in a tone of contemptuous generalisation by a couple of my fellow countrywomen. They had arrived in London in the dog–days, and, lunching at their hotel, had asked to be served with some fruit. The hotel was of the stateliest pattern, and they were waited upon by a functionary whose grandeur was proportionate. This personage bowed and retired, and, after a long delay, reappearing, placed before them with an inimitable gesture a dish of gooseberries and currants. It appeared upon investigation that these acrid vegetables were the only things of succulence that the establishment could undertake to supply; and it seemed to increase the irony of the situation that the establishment was as near as possible to Buckingham Palace. I say that the heroines of my anecdote seemed disposed to generalise: this was sufficiently the case, I mean, to give me a pretext for assuring them that on a thousand fine properties the most beautiful peaches and melons were at that moment ripening either under glass or in warm old walled gardens.

Henry James, *English Hours*, 1905

London's beauty is not in its monuments, but in its immensity; the colossal character of its quays and bridges, The Thames, from London Bridge to Greenwich, I can only compare to an immense moving street of ships, large and small, something suggestive to the Parisian mind of an aquatic Rue de Rivoli. The docks are stupendous buildings, but what impressed me most were the splendid arrangements for unloading vessels, which came close up to the quays, and disembarked their cargoes into the shops, as it were.

Emile Zola

In the autumn of 1900 Mark Twain and his family moved into Brown's Hotel in Dover Street, which inspired Twain to an analysis of the typical London Family hotel:

They are a London speciality, God has not permitted them to exist elsewhere; they are ramshackle clubs which were dwellings at the time of the Heptarchy. Dover and Albemarle Streets are filled with them. The once spacious rooms are split up into coops which afford as much discomfort as can be had anywhere out of jail for any money. All the modern inconveniences are furnished and some that have been obsolete for a century. The prices are astonishingly high for what you get. The bedrooms are hospitals for incurable furniture. I find it so in this one. They exist upon a tradition; they represent the vanishing home-like inn of fifty years ago, and are mistaken by foreigners for it. Some quite respectable Englishmen still frequent them through inherited habit and arrested development; many Americans also, through ignorance and superstition. The rooms are as interesting as the Tower of London, but older I think. Older and dearer. The lift was a gift of William the Conqueror, some of the beds are prehistoric. They represent geological periods. Mine is the oldest. It is formed in strata of Old Red Sandstone, volcanic tufa, ignis fatuus, and bicarbonate of horn-blende, superimposed upon argillaceous shale, and contains the prints of prehistoric man.

Letters from Samuel Clemens to J. Y. M. MacAlister,
1900

Reform Club

... Turgenev proceeded to the Reform Club in Pall Mall. It was here, in Sir Charles Barry's splendid recreation of a Renaissance palace, that he was to breakfast with Bullock Hall. He was pleased to see the latter, and admitted that the venue was magnificent; but he disapproved of the Whiggishness of the place as much as any Tory. He hated the full-length portraits of Palmerston, Lord John Russell and many others on the scagliola walls of the principal hall downstairs, and thought the busts of Cromwell, Richard Cobden and Lord Henry Brougham were if anything more horrible still. And although the Reform Club had once been renowned for its modern services and its exceptional cuisine, he was not much impressed by these either: he was given a meal of baked beans.

Patrick Waddington, *Turgenev and England*, 1980

As Clarence King wrote to John Hay about their friend [Henry James]: 'Whenever he describes the periphery, as anywhere over one cab-fare from his dear Piccadilly, there is a nervous, almost nostalgic, cutting and running for the better quarters of the town. Even when talking of Blackwall or Hampstead, you feel that he looks a little askance, that he wants to go home; and you positively know that before going into these gruesome and out-of-way parts of the town he gathers up a few unmistakably good invitations and buttons them in his inner pocket, so that there should be no mistaking the social position of his corpse if violence befell him.'

Stanley Weintraub, *The London Yankees*, 1979

The City of
Wonderful Nonsense

For the ambitious creative artist, London has always
been a magnet of irresistible power, drawing into its
field so many aspiring virtuosi that, if published reminiscences and memoirs are a reliable guide, the streets
of the town are always likely to be thronged with
hopeful provincials vying with the locals for an entrée
into the Arts. The ambitious young Scot with all his
worldly possessions in one battered trunk, the Irish
émigré doing his hard drinking in the open air, the
colonial adventurer eavesdropping on the small talk
of music-hall matriarchs, the demented Dane with
sadly congested boots, biographers and sculptors who
take advantage of the freemasonry of the trade to insult
their own kind, all have contributed generously to the
mythology of the city they adopted, and which adopted
them.

In March 1885, an unknown writer called James
Matthew Barrie, whose only previous connection with
London had been the submission by post of essays to
magazine editors, arrived on the overnight train from
the north in defiance of professional advice to stay
where he was. The spirit of his arrival proved so
sensational that Barrie could only do justice to it by
removing himself to the third person singular:

Having reached London for the great adventure, he
was hauling his box to the left-luggage shed at St
Pancras when his eyes fell upon what was to him the

most warming sight in literature. It was the placard of the 'St James's Gazette' of the previous evening with printed on it in noble letters 'The Rooks Begin to Build'. This was the title of an article he had sent from Dumfries a few days before. In other dazzling words, having been a minute or so in London, he had made two guineas.

J. M. Barrie, *The Greenwood Hat*, 1937

Dickens to Angela Burdett-Coutts, 1857, on the London visit of Hans Christian Andersen.

We are suffering a good deal from Andersen. His intelligible vocabulary was marvellous. In French or Italian, he was Peter the Wild Boy; in English, the Deaf and Dumb Asylum. My eldest boy swears that the ear of man cannot recognize his German; and his translatress declares to Bentley that he can't speak Danish. In London he got wild entanglements of cabs and Sherry, and never seemed to get out of them again until he was back at Gad's Hill cutting paper into all sorts of patterns and gathering the strangest little nosegays in the woods. One day he came home to Tavistock House, apparently suffering from corns that had ripened in two hours. It turned out that a cab driver had brought him back from the City, by way of the unfinished new thoroughfare through Clerkenwell. Satisfied that the cabman was bent on robbery and murder, he had put his watch and money into his boots – together with a Bradshaw, a pocket-book, a pair of scissors, a penknife, a book or two, a few letters of introduction, and some other miscellaneous property. It was a tremendous business to unpack him and get them off.

(After Andersen had returned home, his host wrote out a memorial notice and affixed it to the Dane's bedroom chest of drawers: 'The great Danish writer Hans Andersen stayed in this room five weeks. And it seemed to the family five years.')

The editorial offices of Ford Madox Ford's English Review.

During the day time, Ford's office was perpetually inundated with visitors, so that it was chiefly at night that the actual job of editing the *Review* could be carried on. But even at night, callers dropped in casually to see how the work was going forward. In order to avoid them, at least for an hour or two, it was Ford's singular practice to attend the second house at the local music-hall. At least once a week my first task, on arriving at Holland Park Avenue, was to secure a box or two stalls at the Shepherd's Bush Empire. After dinner I went out and stopped a hansom and editor and 'sub' drove down to Shepherd's Bush with the manuscripts which had accumulated during the day. During the performance, or rather during the duller turns, Ford made his decisions and I duly recorded them. But when someone really worth listening to – the late Vesta Monks, for example, or Little Tich, or Vesta Victoria – appeared on the stage, the cares of editorship were for the moment laid aside. After the show, we went back to the flat and worked on, sometimes until two in the morning. There must have been a good deal to be said for the Shepherd's Bush Empire from Ford's standpoint. The atmosphere was conducive, there was no one to worry him and he could think undisturbed. When he stayed at home, on the other hand, there was always the prospect of some illuminated friend arriving to drink his whisky and to proffer advice, suggestions or complaints. By contrast, the music-hall must have seemed a haven of peace.

Douglas Goldring, *South Lodge*, 1943

A major Bloomsbury royalty at that time was Lytton Strachey; I knew him but slightly. He made the impression on me of the benevolent demon in the Russian ballet 'Children's Tales' – a demon with a long beard of gardener's bass, and a head which existed only in profile. He seemed to have been cut out of rather thin cardboard. He wasted no words. A young and robustious friend of ours, meeting him at a party, said 'You don't remember me, Mr Strachey. We met four years ago'. 'Quite a nice interval, I think, don't you?', Mr Strachey remarked, pleasantly, and passed on.

Remembering to forget, or, as the Marx brothers put it, 'buying back introductions' was a great feature at the time. It was said – I do not know with what truth – that a certain very great sculptor, on finding the late Mark Gertler at the Café Royal, said to him, 'Gertler, do you remember the time when we were not acquainted?'. Gertler said that he had some dim recollection of it. 'Let us go back to that time, Gertler', said the great man.

I knew Roger Fry well, for I sat to him for several portraits. For one of these, I wore a lily-green evening gown, and my appearance in this, in the full glare of mid-day, and in Fitzroy Square, together with the appearance of Mr Fry, his bushy, rather long grey hair floating from under an enormous black hat, caused great joy to the children of the district as we crossed from Mr Fry's studio to his house for luncheon. Imagining us to be strayed revellers, they inquired at moments (perhaps not unnaturally) if our mothers knew we were out. At other moments they referred to a certain date in November when, according to them, our appearance would have been better timed.

Edith Sitwell, *Coming to London*, 1957

Meantime, I had found me quarters in Villiers Street, Strand, which forty-six years ago was primitive and passionate in its habits and population. My rooms were small, not over-clean or well-kept, but from my desk I could look out of my window through the fan-light of Gatti's Music-Hall entrance, across the street, almost on to its stage. The Charing Cross trains rumbled through my dreams on one side, the boom of the Strand on the other; before my windows, Father Thames under the Shot Tower walked up and down

with his traffic ... My rooms were above an establishment of Harris the Sausage King, who, for tuppence,
gave as much sausage and mash as would carry one
from breakfast to dinner when one dined with nice
people who did not eat sausage for a living. The
excellent tobacco of those days was, unless you sank
to threepenny Shag or soared to sixpenny Turkish,
tuppence the half-ounce; and fourpence, which included
a pewter of beer or porter, was the price of admission
to Gatti's. It was here, in the company of an elderly
but upright barmaid from a pub near by, that I
listened to the observed and compelling songs of the
Lion and Mammoth Comiques, and the shriller strains –
but equally 'observed' – of the Bessies and Bellas,
whom I could hear arguing beneath my window with
their cab drivers, as they sped from Hall to Hall. One
lady sometimes delighted us with *viva-voce* versions of
– 'what 'as just 'appened to me outside 'ere, if you'll
believe it'. Then she would plunge into brilliant
improvisations. Oh, we believed! Many of us had,
perhaps, taken part in the tail of that argument at the
doors, ere she stormed in.

Rudyard Kipling, *Something of Myself*, 1937

*One of the greatest of all black-and-white artists, and a
specialist in the delineation of London low life, was
Philip William May (1864–1903), a completely self-
taught master plagued by a frail constitution which
soon collapsed under the weight of conviviality imposed
upon it. May's glory was his economy of line. Once,
when an editor crassly complained that his drawings
were not finished up, May replied, 'When I can leave
out half the lines I now use, I shall want six times
the money'.*

May worked very fast and would execute a delayed
commission while the messenger waited for it. He
squandered his vast earnings on cadgers and the in-
valuable originals of his drawings were given away
and lost, though sometimes, after one of his Sunday

afternoon receptions, Mrs May would visit the guests and try to get back from them the drawings her husband had pressed them to take. He was usually paid in advance and never had any money, though he could always get a fiver at the *Sketch* by doing a drawing at the counter and cashing it like a cheque.

May drank heavily but not bitterly. He was a kindly, sociable person. Though he looked like a stable lad, he was much more musical than horsey. His face was deadly pale. He had beautiful hands. He lived in a fever of Nineties Bohemianism. Though he has been linked more with the 'Pink 'Un' than the 'Yellow Book' he was in fact a witty and intelligent lover of the arts. If London's Bohemia was genuinely the meeting place of the artistic and the raffish, May was one of the very few true Bohemians of the period. He died of a wasting disease caused by early malnutrition and hard drinking. At his death he weighed five stone. He was only thirty-nine and in the light of that some of the stories are not quite so funny – Mrs May's waking up in the morning to find the hansom-cabby sleeping in the bed too, and all the rest.

R. G. G. Price, A *History of Punch*, 1957

Maiden Lane at this time of year is the only place where an enormous percentage of the men are heroes, and of the women heroines. There is a Roman Catholic church at the corner, which was more used before the Irish colony was driven out of Clare Market, and to come into the lane at this end is perhaps the most suitable introduction. But there is a great deal to be said for coming at it from one of the alleys – cracks between houses – which lead up from the Strand. The chief beauty of these alleys after dark is the way they are illuminated by concealed lights filtering out from windows which you cannot see till you come up to them. Going up one alley, I looked in at a lighted window, and beheld a bicycle repairer at work among such a litter of iron as one might expect to see in a

St. James, Garlick Hill

village shop. He worked under a flare of gas. I was so astonished to see him and his shop – I felt as though I were looking in at the forge of a village blacksmith – that I stood and gazed. He came to me and said: 'If you go up to the top and turn to the left, you will get out'. I did not want to get out in the least, but I obeyed his instructions. I suppose the people who dwell in these cracks think that every stranger who comes there has got in by mistake, and that the true hospitality of the quarter is to show him out. But this only deepens the mystery of the bicycle repairer. Why does he repair bicycles in this spot, if, when a possible customer comes, he only runs out and says, 'Go up to the top and turn to the left'?

Maiden Lane, I said, is frequented by heroes and heroines. The heroines may also be heroes, as this happens in pantomime. Maiden Lane is also the only place where I ever heard of prosperous people in fur coats stopping their conversation when a policeman comes in sight, politely whistling 'A Policeman's Lot is not a Happy One' and gravely continuing their conversation when the policeman has passed on. There is an excellent tea-shop in Maiden Lane, and here the principal boys, principal girls, star-trap jumpers (first-grade – and there are not many left), high-class demons, and the most important fairies congregate. I think the waitresses brighten their occupation by temporary incursions into pantomime. You can hire rooms in this lane to drill a chorus. There are also rooms for fitting on pantomime clothes. Here too is Rule's saloon, full of ancient prints, cartoons, and theatrical reminiscences. Round the walls are little shrines, where electric light illumines the busts of Charles Mathews and Dan Leno, and the figures of Hyperides and Phryne. Hyperides, having failed to clear Phryne of a charge of impiety, is indicating to the judges the beauty of his client, for all the world like a French lawyer.

J. B. Atkins, *Side Shows*, 1908

I found in Curzon Street another 'Nouvelle Athenes', a Bohemianism of titles that went back to the Conquest, a Bohemianism of the ten sovereigns always a-jingle in the trousers pocket, of scrupulous cleanliness, of hansom cabs, of ladies' pet names; of triumphant champagne, of debts, gaslight, supper-parties, morning light, coaching a fabulous Bohemianism; a Bohemianism of eternal hardupishness and eternal squandering of money – money that rose at no discoverable well-head and flowed into a sea of boudoirs and restaurants, a sort of whirlpool of sovereigns in which we were caught, and sent eddying through music-halls, bright shoulders, tresses of hair, and slang; and I joined in the adorable game of Bohemianism that was played round and about Piccadilly Circus, with Curzon Street for a magnificent rallying point. After dinner a general 'clear' was made in the directions of halls and theatres, a few friends would drop in around twelve, and continue their drinking till three or four; but Saturday night was gala night – at half-past eleven the lords drove up in their hansoms, then a genius or two would arrive, and supper and singing went merrily until the chimney sweeps began to go by. Then we took chairs and bottles into the street and entered into discussion with the policemen. Twelve hours later we struggled out of our beds, and to the sound of church bells we commenced writing.

George Moore, *Confessions of a Young Man*, 1886

SYMPHONY IN YELLOW

> An omnibus across the bridge
> Crawls like a yellow butterfly,
> And, here and there, a passer-by
> Shows like a little restless midge.
>
> Big barges full of yellow hay
> Are moored against the shadowy wharf,
> And, like a yellow silken scarf,
> The thick fog hangs along the quay.
>
> The yellow leaves begin to fade
> And flutter from the Temple elms,
> And at my feet the pale green Thames
> Lies like a rod of rippled jade.

Oscar Wilde

I was beginning to enjoy being about in London. I had grown up looking on it as a place whose grime and noisiness made one doubly thankful for living in the country. But there came a moment during that summer when I realized that I was acquiring a liking for its back-street smells and busy disregard of my existence. Walking home at night I began to be quite fond of Holborn, and I became aimlessly attached to certain places merely through passing them so often. I was learning to love the city breezes; the country thoughts they carried with them gave the town intensity, and taught one the value of its trees. The skies had never meant so much to me as they did now in dingy London. Sunsets beyond those roofs and chimneys, those miles of bricks and mortar, affected me with a newly-discovered emotion, inexpressible and alluring with the vague regrets of my ignorant 'twenties. There was a sort of poetry behind it all which fed my mind and created stirrings of expectation.

Siegfried Sassoon, *The Weald of Youth*, 1942

A Metropolitan Miscellany

In the course of its long, crowded life, London has given rise to as many tall stories, curious anecdotes, sad glimpses of hidden lives, whimsicalities and absurdities as there have been people who passed through its streets. The nostalgic and the outrageous, the poetic and the prosaic, the painfully accurate and the patently invented, impress themselves through fragments of biography and reminiscence.

Of Cleopatra's Needle:

In 1878 sealed jars were placed under the obelisk containing a man's lounge suit, the complete dress and vanities of a woman of fashion, illustrated papers, Bibles in many languages, children's toys, a razor, cigars, photographs of the most beautiful women of Victorian England, and a complete set of coinage from a farthing to five pounds. So the most ancient monument in London stands guard over this modernity, rather like an experienced old hen, waiting for Time to hatch it.

H. V. Morton, *The Heart of London*, 1925

Children of Stepney were using the whole of the Rotherhithe Tunnel as a loudspeaker, their shrill voices trumpeting and turmoiling through the tubes and vaults of the long strange underway. Night had subdued the thunder of traffic, and as we journeyed from South London to Wapping by way of the tunnel, we went by dark, deserted ways and saw streets named after Paradise and Cathay. The tunnel was empty and presented a vista of continuous electric lights, trailing their gleams like comets' tails. Its white-tiled roof stretched on ahead of us and lost itself in a grey haze. One had the feeling of making a passage from world to world. The Thames flowed above our heads, but we did not hear it; all London was about us, but was invisible. All we heard were children afar trying their voices in a way that sounded like the cries of lost souls. The great day-traffic of the tunnel was gone, and now in its place mournful-looking couples walked slowly along the footway. A man came towards us with two carpenter's sacks on his shoulders, but he said not a word as he passed. He looked like Pilgrim and his burden of sin.

Spiral staircases, however, rose up at points, and the roof gave way to what looked like watchtowers, and, standing under these great vents, one could look up all the way to the stars. As we paused under one of them and listened, we heard as from a great distance church bells tolling mysteriously and dismally. Surely this tunnel, where little boys in red jackets sweep up after horses by day and the air is full of smokes and steams and gigantic sounds, is one of the queerest places in London, as strange by night as it is unwonted by day.

While we waited at a bend near mid-tunnel, came a sound that scared us and raised the hair on our heads and bid us almost hold on to one another in fright. It was like oncoming hell and the destruction of humanity at large. Some gigantic force was approaching, driving all before it, but ahead of it came armies of yelling fiends, clearing a course, smashing and blinding and destroying. What a nightmare sound! Truly, nightmare merely; for it proved nothing more fearsome than a belated empty Ford van passing from North to South London. When it had passed it was like doom having passed us. Its long and dreadful retreat gave way to silence and whispering and the renewed calling of church bells and unseen children trying their voices and echoes somewhere far off.

Stephen Graham, *London Nights*, 1925

We talk of men keeping dogs, but we might often talk more expressively of dogs keeping men. I know a bull-dog in a shy corner of Hammersmith who keeps a man. He keeps him up a yard, and makes him go to public houses and lay wagers on him, and obliges him to lean against posts and look at him, and forces him to neglect work for him, and keeps him under rigid coercion.

Charles Dickens, *The Uncommercial Traveller*, 1861

Consider the following advertisement in the *West London Observer* for 18th August in that very year, 1910:

Six-roomed houses redecorated, thoroughly done, twenty shillings. Ceilings from two shillings. Walker, 35, Godolphin Road, auxiliary postman.

And here are some housing rents and values as they appear in comparable advertisements in the same newspaper:

Furnished flat, sitting room, two bedrooms, separate kitchen, piano, plate and linen. One guinea weekly. 5, Brooklyn Road, Shepherd's Bush.
Room, furnished, suit married couple, everything for use, five shillings per week. 11, Crisp Road, Hammersmith.
Six-roomed house £195, 75-year lease, near trams; bargain. Only wants seeing.

Indeed, houses with 99-year leases and the offer of the freehold were commonly selling at £200. A year or two later there appeared this advertisement in the same paper:

Why pay rent when you can buy one of the splendidly appointed houses on the Crabtree Estate in the Fulham Palace Road? Each contains pretty entrance hall, two sitting-rooms, three bedrooms, bathroom and scullery. Roofs boarded and tiled, bathroom tiled, electric light fittings supplied throughout, blinds fitted to all front windows. 99-year lease. Ground rent £6. Freehold can be had. Price – £300, of which only £35 need be paid down.

Whitehall Gardens

Yet my parents and their intimates, I remember, thought these were totally impossible prices, putting house-ownership far beyond the reach of such as they. The Crabtree Estate, it was said, was 'all too fancy', with its built-in electric light fixtures and its fitted blinds. The electric lighting in particular was all very well, but it 'impaired one's eyesight'. I remember the phrase so well, for it set me wondering what other kind of sight there was. The Crabtree Estate, must, we thought, have been getting a huge subvention from the electric-lighting companies, upstarts who were bent on doing us all out of our beloved gaslight at all costs. Our landlord never succumbed; we never had electric light until we lived in the City.

C. H. Rolph, *London Particulars*, 1980

Of Walter de la Mare:

Reverting to the Athenaeum, he said that he once went into the club during the war, when it was all shored up, and he was entirely alone. He felt that he must break a rule, so he lit a cigarette in the drawing-room before one o'clock. I asked him if he knew T. B. Strong, a former Dean of Christ Church, Oxford, who frequented the club a good deal, and was said, when he was an old man, occasionally to gate a waiter in the absent-minded belief that he was still at Oxford.

Russell Brain, *Tea With Walter de la Mare*, 1942

Two cornet performances have left an abiding memory with me. One was M. Levy's variation on 'Yankee Doodle', taken *prestissimo*...The other was 'The Pilgrim of Love', played by an itinerant artist outside a public house in Clipstone Street, Portland Place. The man played with great taste and pathos; but, to my surprise, he had no knowledge of musical etiquette, for when, on his holding his hat to me for a donation, I explained that I was a member of the press, he still seemed to expect me to pay for my entertainment, a shocking instance of popular ignorance.

G. B. Shaw, *The Star*, March, 1889

THOUGHTS ON 'THE DIARY OF A NOBODY'

The Pooters walked to Watney Lodge
One Sunday morning hot and still
Where public footpaths used to dodge
Round elms and oaks to Muswell Hill.

That burning buttercuppy day
The local dogs were curled in sleep,
The writhing trunks of flowery May
Were polished by the sides of sheep.

And only footsteps in a lane
And birdsong broke the silence round
And chuffs of the Great Northern train
For Alexandra Palace bound.

The Watney Lodge I seem to see
Is gabled gothic hard and red,
With here a monkey-puzzle tree
And there a round geranium bed.

Each mansion, each new-planted pine,
Each short and ostentatious drive
Mean Morning Prayer and beef and wine
And Queen Victoria alive.

Dear Charles and Carrie, I am sure,
Despite that awkward Sunday dinner,
Your lives were good and more secure
Than ours at cocktail time in Pinner.

John Betjeman

Gamage's 3-horsepower motor cycles, first sold in 1902, claimed to 'beat the flower of both English and foreign makes of often double the hp'. When he died, Walter Gamage was laid in state in the Motoring Department, with members of the staff mounting guard at the catafalque day and night.

Alison Adburgham, *Shopping in Style*, 1979

The statistical approach to metropolitan problems was one of several weapons in the armoury of Henry Mayhew (1812–87), whose disclosures of life below the poverty line were so devastating that they inspired Thackeray to guilt-racked enthusiasm:

What a confession it is that we have all of us been obliged to make! A clever and earnest-minded writer gets a commission, and reports upon the state of our poor in London: he goes amongst labouring people and poor of all kinds – and brings back what? A picture of human life so wonderful, so awful, so piteous and pathetic, so exciting and terrible, that readers of romance own they never read anything like it; and that the griefs, struggles, strange adventures here depicted exceed anything that any of us could imagine.

Thackeray wrote those thoughts down in 1850, when Mayhew's reports began appearing in the Morning Chronicle. *But as early as 1837 the rising Boz had already reduced the statistical method to wonderful absurdity by correlating dogs'–meat with Her*

Majesty's Navy. Nobody, however, was more closely acquainted with statistical folly than Mayhew himself, who grew up under the tutelage of a father who lost so many umbrellas in his daily journeys to and from home to office, Fitzroy Square to Carey Street, that he purchased new umbrellas by the gross as a means of reducing expenditure.

There are in round numbers 300,000 inhabited houses in the metropolis; and allowing the married people living in apartments to be equal in number to the unmarried 'housekeepers', we may compute that the number of families in London is about the same as the inhabited houses. Assuming one young or old gentleman in every ten of these families to smoke one cigar per diem in the public thoroughfares, we have 30,000 cigar-ends daily, or 210,000 weekly cast away in the London streets. Now, reckoning 150 cigars to go to a pound, we may assume that each end so cast away weighs about the thousandth part of a pound; consequently the gross weight of the end flung into the gutter will, in the course of the week, amount to about 2 cwt; and calculating that only a sixth part of these are picked up by the finders, it follows that there is very nearly a ton of refuse tobacco collected annually in the metropolitan thoroughfares.

Henry Mayhew, *London Labour and the London Poor*, 1861–2

Mr Slug then stated some curious calculations respecting the dogs'-meat barrows of London. He found that the total number of small carts and barrows engaged in dispensing provision to the cats and dogs of the metropolis was 1,743. The average number of skewers delivered daily with the provender, by each dogs'-meat cart to barrow, was thirty-six. Now, multiplying the number of skewers so delivered by the number of barrows, a total of 62,748 skewers daily would be obtained. Allowing that, of these 62,748 skewers, the odd 2,748 were accidentally devoured with the meat,

by the most voracious of the animals supplied, it followed that 60,000 skewers per day, or the enormous
number of 21,900,000 skewers annually, were wasted
in the kennels and dustholes of London; which, if
collected and warehoused, would in ten years' time
afford a mass of timber more than sufficient for the
construction of a first-rate vessel of war for the use of
her Majesty's navy, to be called 'The Royal Skewer',
and to become under that name the terror of all the
enemies of this island.

Charles Dickens, 'The Mudfog Papers' from
Sketches by Boz, 1837

Saturday, December 7, 1850:

We called at Millais's, having engaged to see his
picture and design, but found we had overstayed our
time. However, I met him almost immediately, parading
Tottenham Court Road, together with Hunt and
Collins, on the search for models. They found one or
two women adaptable for Millais – the best being in
company of two men; but did not muster face to
address them, with the likelihood of a cry of 'Police'.

William Michael Rossetti, *The PRB Journal*,
1849–1853

During the first ten years at Tudor House Rossetti
entertained constantly and lavishly; but there is an
impression, in letters and descriptions, that the house
was badly run, untidy, and not over-clean. Servants
came and went; we hear of rats and mice in the studio,
and William Allingham found a mouse eating a kipper
in the basement . . . The collecting of 'wild beasts' was
a craze which began soon after Rossetti arrived in
Cheyne Walk. He had always been fascinated by odd
creatures, a taste shared by his sister Christina, whose
goblins in 'Goblin Market' with their 'demure grimaces'
have faces 'cat-like and rat-like, Ratel and wombat-
like'. Wombats had for Gabriel an irresistible charm,
and he installed one at Tudor House. There is a pencil
drawing at the Tate Gallery by William Bell Scott

entitled 'Rossetti's Wombat Seated on His Lap'. Only the hand of the master appears but the fat, chuckling creature is faithfully depicted, drinking out of a cup – an endearing beast with a figure not unlike Rossetti's in middle life. This animal is said to have devoured the new straw hat of a patroness called Mrs Virtue Tebbs while she sat for her portrait. When it was discovered, 'Oh, poor wombat!', cried Rossetti, 'it is so indigestible'.

In the garden Rossetti kept peacocks, and built wooden sheds to house armadilloes and kangaroos. There were squirrels, mice, and dormice, and two owls called Jessie and Bobbie. There was a racoon.

Jeffry Dunn describes his introduction to this beast, which was imprisoned in a packing-case under a heavy slab of marble. When the lid was heaved up, Rossetti 'put his hand in quickly, seized the "coon" by the scruff of its neck, hauled it out, and held it up, in a plunging, kicking, teeth-showing state for me to look at, remarking, "Does it not look like a devil?", to which I agreed'.

This creature was constantly gnawing its way out of captivity, paying nocturnal visits to a neighbour's chicken-house and eating the eggs, for which outlawry Rossetti eventually received a bill. The racoon was sent back to the man he bought it from. Rossetti had a curious attitude to animals, treating them either as specimens to admire or as comical toys; but never apparently bestowing much thought upon their comfort in captivity. They were displayed enthusiastically for the entertainment of guests, one of whom, Miss Ellen Terry, gives several accounts of the Cheyne Walk menagerie.

'He bought a white bull because it had eyes like Janey Morris, and tethered it on the lawn ... Soon there was no lawn left, only the bull. He invited people to meet it, and heaped favours on it, until it kicked everything to pieces, when he reluctantly got rid of it.' His zoo must have been a sad disappointment to

him: there were so many casualties. The young
kangaroo murdered his mother and was in turn
slaughtered – it was thought by the racoon. A white
peacock, released on arrival in the drawing-room, dived
under a sofa, where it remained, refusing to move,
for several days.

'The lovely creature won't respond to me', said
Rossetti pathetically to a friend.

The friend dragged out the bird.

'No wonder! It's dead!'

'He tried to repair the failure', continued Miss Terry,
'by buying some white dormice. He sat them up on
tiny bamboo chairs, and they looked sweet ... If the
animals didn't die they annoyed the neighbours. The
armadilloes disappeared, burrowing their way into other
people's gardens, where they threw up heaps of earth
and ruined the flower beds. One, more adventurous,
burrowed under a neighbour's house and came up
through the kitchen floor, sending the cook into
screaming hysterics. The beautiful fallow deer pursued
the peacock, trampling on its tail till all the feathers
came out; the peacock flew up into the trees, calling its
mate with piercing shrieks. Neighbours complained, and
the Cadogen Estate inserted a clause in the leases of
Cheyne Walk houses, which remains to this day, forbidding the keeping of peacocks.

Thea Holme, *Chelsea*, 1972

The first railway escalator in London was brought into
use on 4 October 1911, at Earl's Court, between the
Piccadilly and District Lines, but in the early days
many members of the public mistrusted it. A man
with a wooden leg, called 'Bumper' Harris, was therefore engaged to travel up and down all day to give
passengers confidence.

Charles E. Lee, *The Piccadilly Line; A Brief History*,
1973

What I miss most of London's vanished colour are the
window-boxes which, from the beginning of May to

the end of July, marked the Season. Marguerites and geraniums, lobelias and calceolarias from top to bottom of every house from Kensington to Mayfair. White and red and pink and blue and yellow. And in the dusk the smell of the fresh-watered earth wafted along the stale streets, the very staleness of which had a half-sweet rustic smell in those days when horses drew the traffic. That smell will never return. It has vanished with the smell of the oranges and the gas in Drury Lane Theatre, with the perfume of the lavender cried at the end of our summer holidays by girls in grey shawls and big hats, with the smell of the dust laid by leisurely watering-carts on a fine May morning, and with the scent of the musk that once upon a time made fragrant the dingiest room in the dingiest slum, but which now all the world over is scentless.

Compton Mackenzie, *Echoes*, 1954

The Savage Club itself had departed months before, but some of its staunchest members haunted the old quarters until the housebreakers' men, they say, removed most of them. The Club's last Saturday night dinner was a sad, sentimental affair. The big front room was so packed that the soloists had to sing in their seats. There was at the dinner an auction sale. The pineapple (presented by Dr Livingstone in 1884) and a few other relics were sold by auction, the chairman knocking them down with the Club's big knobkerrie.

At midnight the chairman asked for silence. The lights went out, the scratching needle of a gramophone could be heard, and suddenly voices from the past came through the mist of blue smoke – old Odell's quavering voice in 'We'll Welcome the Harvest Home', Albert Chevalier in 'My Old Dutch', Lords Roberts and Jellicoe (snatches from speeches), Charles Santley in 'Simon the Cellarer' (a member from behind the stub of a cigar impaled on a toothpick murmured, 'I accompanied Charles in that'), a selection from Elgar's

'Requiem' ended the Savage records. The lights went up. 'Auld Lang Syne' was wailed.

Time to go. The Savages spread into the Terrace. It was March but the night was like June, yet everyone seemed to be looking older although they sang snatches of song as they walked. So the Club went west, past the Athenaeum to its new house which had once been the home of Lord Curzon himself in Carlton House Terrace. And the ghosts of the Club's forty-five years drifted with them. The Club laureate had mind of them and in his menu poem that night had written:

> Where these dear ghosts we love the best
> Will know exactly how to find us.
> We mustn't leave our ghosts behind us.

James Bone, *London Echoing*, 1948

I used to have violin lessons from the queer, tragic Borschitzky, whose dismal adventure caused Euston Square to be re-christened. He came home late at night and found his landlady murdered in the kitchen. Being nearly blind he fell over the body, got himself covered with blood and as a foreigner and a musician was at once arrested by the intelligent police. He was of course acquitted but the trial caused so much sensation as 'The Euston Square murder' that the respectable inhabitants petitioned to have the name of the square changed and it become Endsleigh Gardens.

Ford Madox Ford, *Return to Yesterday*, 1932

A London of horse-trams with halfpenny fares, and of hansom cabs; of crystalline bells and spattering hoofs. A London with winters of slush and fog of a richer sort than any known today, and summers of dust and clam; the slush and the dust being its heritage from the horse-traffic. A London of silk hats, frock-coats, beards, curled moustaches, choker collars, leg-of-mutton sleeves, veils, bonnets and, threading through these gigmanities as herald of revolt, an execrated vixen in bloomers riding a bicycle. A London of solid homes, which regarded the introduction of flat-life as something Not Quite Nice... A London of low buildings ... of lost corners; of queer nooks and rookeries (slums of little jerry-built houses with only narrow alleys between them); of curling lanes and derelict squares ... A London which, away from the larger streets, held pools of utter darkness and terraces of crumbling caverns... A London whose roads were mainly granite setts and therefore a London of turmoil and clatter. A London which was the centre of an empire and knew it. And a London which, in a few of its nerves, was beginning to be aware of the end of an epoch and of the new this and the new that.

Thomas Burke, *London in my Time*, 1934

No London child today can realize the quiet of the road on which my window looked. A tradesman's cart, a hawker or a hurdy-gurdy, were the sum total of the usual traffic. Sometimes everything had been so quiet for so long that the sound of a passer-by or of a butcher's pony would take on a distant, unreal tone, as if it were mocking me. This frightened me, and I would break the spell by singing 'The Lass of Richmond Hill'.

Molly Hughes, *A London Child of the Seventies*, 1943

War & its Aftermath

During the Second World War, certain amendments were imposed both on the landscape of London and on the lives of its inhabitants. For a while after that war, siege conditions continued to prevail for a period of time which foreigners sometimes found irritating. In the end peace was taken for granted once more, but London was not the same city which had gone into the war. It was changed beyond recall, improved in some ways, despoiled in others. It began consciously to ape its own past in an orgy of nostalgic yearning. Not only had other great cities overtaken it in size, in wealth, in population, in significance, but it seemed unconcerned by its demotion. Perhaps it has never recognized it.

The Great Blitz of Wednesday April 16.

This was the worst raid Central London had ever experienced. The sirens which usually don't go before ten went at nine. I was drinking with Dorothy Glover, in the Horseshoe. We went out and tried to get dinner. Corner House full, Frascati's closed. Victor's closed. At the York Minster the chef was about to go home. Ended in the Czardas in Dean Street. Sitting next the plate-glass windows we felt apprehensive. By ten it was obvious that this was a real blitz. Bomb bursts – perhaps the ones in Piccadilly – shook the restaurant. Left at ten-thirty and walked back to Gower Mews. Wished I had my steel helmet. Changed, and went out with D, who was firewatching. Standing on the roof of a garage we saw the flares come slowly floating down, dribbling their flames: they drift like great yellow peonies.

At midnight reported at the post and went out on the north side. At a quarter to two nothing had happened in the district, and I planned to sign off at two-thirty. Then the flares came down again right on top of us, as the Pole, Miss S, of Bourne and Hollingsworth, and I stood in Tottenham Court Road at the corner of Alfred Place. A white southern light: we cast long shadows and the flares came down from west to east across Charlotte Street. Then a few minutes later, without the warning of a whistle, there was a huge detonation. We only had time to get on our haunches and the shop window showered down on our helmets.

Ran down Alfred Place. A light shone out in a top flat at the corner of Ridgemount Gardens: we shouted at it and ran on – the windows must have been blasted. Then confusion. Gower Street on both sides seemed ravaged. Never realised the parachute bomb had fallen behind on the Victoria Club in Malet Street where 350 Canadian soldiers were sleeping. Women bleeding from cuts on the face in dressing-gowns said there was someone hurt on the top floor above RADA. Two other wardens and a policeman – we ran up four littered flights. Girl on the floor. Bleeding. Stained pyjamas. Her hip hurt. Only room for one man to lift her at a time. Very heavy. Took her over for two flights, but she had to be changed three times. In pain, but she apologised for being heavy. Stretcher party came down and took her away from the ground floor. All down Gower Street they came out in their doorways – many unhurt, but so many bleeding in a superficial way in squalid pyjamas grey with debris dust. These were the casualties of glass. Confusion. Not enough stretcher parties. Went back to post and the blackout boards blew out and we went down on the floor. Out again to find something to do. That was the odd difficulty. Jacobs had become Incident Officer with a blue light beside him at the corner of Gower Street and Keppel Street. This was indeed local and domestic war like something out of 'The Napoleon of Notting Hill'.

Graham Greene, *Ways of Escape*, 1980

I stayed for a time at the Hyde Park Hotel, which still managed to keep up the appearances of a Victorian comfort and grandeur. The waiter asked me what I wanted to order for breakfast in my room the next morning. When, in reciting the meager menu, he mentioned scrambled eggs and sausages, I said, 'That's fine! – bring me that'. 'That's not what they usually say when they see it, sir', he dampeningly replied. I should have done well to take his warning, for, when my breakfast came, the eggs turned out to be concoctions of egg-powder, and I saw what someone had meant when he told me that sausages in England were now a form of bread.

Edmund Wilson, *Europe Without Baedeker*, 1947

I am old enough to have known three distinctive periods of London life. I have ridden in a horse tram. I have been run over by a hansom cab. I have heard the muffin bell and watched those scores of London hopeful lads, dressed in white jackets by the London County Council, running into the traffic to brush up the horse manure. I have lived through the raffish, revolutionary, angry London of the twenties and thirties, watched that identifiable thread of single workless figures mooching, twenty yards apart and not speaking to one another, from shop window to shop window: the unemployed. Street singers still made the London Sunday afternoon a misery at that time. And in the spiritless streets of Bloomsbury the 'window bang' seller used to traipse by on windy days, offering us those sausages of cloth to put on our window-sashes to keep out the ruling fiend of London life: the draught. (Meteorologists point out that it is true to call the London climate windy rather than rainy.) And then –

if it is possible for anyone over the age of thirty-five to know it – I have known the gaudy birth of contemporary London, the affluent.

V. S. Pritchett, *London Perceived*, 1962

They dined together at an oldish French restaurant in Soho, rather smelly and over-furnished and decorated in a Nineties style, as if it expected Toulouse Lautrec to come creeping in at any moment.

J. B. Priestley, *London End*, 1968

London no longer belongs to the 'nobs' and the 'toffs'; it belongs to the crowd. If the 'nobs' no longer go to their clubs, but turn up in the Chelsea pubs, they are careful to put on their pull-overs, their cavalry twill, their unsporting sporting clothes. The crowd has set the tone. The once silent squares in the centre fill up every night with motor coaches that bring trippers from the provinces by tens of thousands. They come to bathe in neon, and London drains the life from all England. A city like Manchester is dead after seven. The crowd rolls into the pubs and the coffee bars where it is waited on by Cypriots, Italians and Germans. It pushes into the strip-tease clubs and the clip joints where the girls claim to be hospital nurses by day and, in fact, often are. The notorious swarm of prostitutes has been driven off the streets and relies on small ads in shop windows offering massage, dancing lessons, modelling; they signal from windows. Lately they are venturing once more into doorways. Popular taste runs less to the old London gaudiness and loudness than to Edwardian or Regency chichi. Many of the new 'democratic' pubs where the separate bars have been abolished are dolled up with arty iron and glass work, coloured glasses, artificial flowers, fake Toby jugs, plushy wall-papers, and chains of coloured lights. Thank heaven there are plenty of simple places, in the old varnish and mahogany, some with the beautifully etched Victorian glass and lettering, where one meets the old mild pomposities, where one can be reassured by an aspidistra and a stout barmaid who calls you 'love' or 'dear' and overfeeds her dog.

And in the common London of the buses, cheap, shops, bars, you are always 'dear' or 'love'. It is all 'What's yours, love?' 'Where to, dear?' 'Here you are, ducks' to man, woman, or child. One lives in an ooze of affection. But hard, sharp-eyed, kind, sentimental London always keeps its head and, in a crisis, resorts at once to the stern mask of respectability. I know nothing more indicative of the London temper than the change in the faces, the shocked silence, the look of moral *de haut en bas* that comes over any collection of us when, publicly, 'something' happens. 'Something' absolutely must *not* happen in this room, office, cinema, bar, street. We are appalled – unless, of course, the 'something' has happened to a dog, and then all our passion is roused and, in chorus, we go mad and address the whole world with indignation. Until someone utters that healing moral phrase that must be spoken a million times a day on the London streets and that will instantly cure our panic: 'It's wrong. It's not right. It's all wrong'. Except in the matter of what happens to dogs, cats, horses, budgerigars, and canaries, London is the least nervous city in the world.

V. S. Pritchett, *London Perceived*, 1962

As it was in the Beginning

The student of London's affairs ends as he started, confronted by the irrepressible hunger for and appreciation of, London life which animates those who count themselves as her citizens. Some of the most passionate Londoners have been the provincials who tried to maintain a shrewd disinterest and thankfully failed. Others have been writers who were born, who lived and died within the metropolitan limits. Some have been foreign expatriates who could never quite tear themselves away. All of them had in common one quality, an intensity of affection for London, a degree of reliance on its stimulus, a sense of wonder unabated in its sheer bewildering complexity.

London that eternally thrills me and has been to me all the bright wishes of my youth conceived.

J. M. Barrie, 1937

We may hurry across the great stretches and folds of a park, with a glamorous smirched sunset, curling clouds over the distant houses, wisps of mist becoming palpably blue against the thorn-trees, and the call of a closing space and of a closing in day, indescribably mournful and distant. We may hurry to our triumph of love, to our bankruptcy, to our end or our beginning of the world. Or we may be driven behind a slipping, frightened horse through the gray empty streets, among whirls of small hard snowflakes, to a house where there are the titter and bustle of a wedding, or where on the stairs there are the heavy footfalls and muffled breathings of men carrying down the coffin of our best friend in the world. The background for either mood will be the right one. It is these things that come back to us at a distance and in odd ways. I have known a man, dying a long way from London, sigh queerly for a sight of the gush of smoke that, on the platform of the Underground, one may see, escaping in great woolly clots up a circular opening, by a grimy, rusted iron shield, into the dim upper light. He wanted to see it again as others have wished to see once more the Bay of Naples, the olive groves of Catania. Another wanted – how very much he wanted! – to see once more the sort of carpet of pigeons on the gravel in front of a certain Museum steps; the odd top-hatted unpresentable figure of a battered man, holding a paper of bun crumbs, with pigeons on his shoulders, on his hands, crowding in between his feet and fluttering like an aureole of wings round his head.

London is a thing of these 'bits'. It is seldom that one sees at one time as much of it as one may always see of any country town. It has nothing, it never had anything, worth talking of as a spectacular expression of humanity of that incongruous jumble of races that is England. It has no Acropolis, no Forum Romanum, no Champs Elysées; it has not so much as a Capitol or a Nevski Prospekt. The tombs of its Kings, its Valhalla, its Senate, are, relatively to London, nowhere in particular. Viewed from a distance it is a cloud on the horizon. From the dark, further side of the Surrey hills at night, above the inky skyline of heather, of pine tops, of elms, one may see on the sky a brooding and sinister glow. That is London – manifesting itself on the clouds.

Ford Madox Ford, *The Soul of London*

Go where we may – rest where we will,
Eternal London haunts us still.

Thomas Moore, from *Rhymes on the Road*, 1820

London is so clumsy and so brutal, and has gathered together so many of the darkest sides of life, that it is almost ridiculous to talk of her as a lover talks of his mistress, and almost frivolous to appear to ignore her disfigurements and cruelties. She is like a mighty ogress who devours human flesh; but to me it is a mitigating circumstance – though it may not seem so to every one – that the ogress herself is human. It is not in wantonness that she fills her maw, but to keep herself alive and do her tremendous work. She has no time for fine discriminations, but after all she is as good-natured as she is huge, and the more you stand up to her, as the phrase is, the better she takes the joke of it. It is mainly when you fall on your face before her that she gobbles you up. She heeds little what she takes, so long as she has her stint, and the smallest push to the right or the left will divert her wavering bulk from one form of prey to another. It is not to be denied that the heart tends to grow hard in her company; but she is a capital antidote to the morbid, and to live with her successfully is an education of the temper, a consecration of one's private philosophy. She gives one a surface for which in a rough world one can never be too thankful. She may take away reputations, but she forms character. She teaches her victims not to 'mind', and the great danger for them is perhaps that they shall learn the lesson too well.

Henry James, *English Hours*, 1905

The difficulty of going at what I call a rapid pace, is prodigious; it is almost an impossibility. I suppose this is partly the effect of two years ease, and partly of the absence of streets and of numbers of figures. I can't express how much I want these. It seems as if they supplied something to my brain, which it cannot bear, when busy, to lose. For a week or a fortnight I can write prodigiously in a retired place, as at Broadstairs, and a day in London sets me up again and starts me.

But the toil and labour of writing, day after day, without that magic lantern, is IMMENSE!

Charles Dickens, Letter to John Forster,
30 August 1846

'Being a Londoner, and incapable of reverence...'

Frank Swinnerton, *Background with Chorus*, 1956

Afterword

For all the enchantments and fascinations it has to offer, is London necessary? The Wiltshire writer-naturalist Richard Jefferies (1848–87), who began this anthology by suggesting that London was the only real place in the world, now ends it with the diametrically opposed proposition that there are those who prefer Wiltshire:

The old house stood by the silent country road, secluded by many a long, long mile, and yet again secluded within the great walls of the garden. Often and often I rambled up to the milestone which stood under an oak, to look at the chipped inscription low down – 'To London, 79 miles'. So far away, you see, that the very inscription was cut at the foot of the stone, since no man would be likely to want that information.

'*Meadow Thoughts*', from *The Life of the Fields*,
1884

✦ Acknowledgements ✦

The editor and publisher gratefully acknowledge permission to use copyright material in this book:

Alison Adburgham: From *Shopping in Style* (1979). Reprinted by permission of Thames & Hudson Ltd.

J. B. Atkins: From *Side Shows* (1908). Reprinted by permission of Jonathan Cape Ltd., for the author.

J. M. Barrie: From *The Greenwood Hat* (Peter Davies, 1937). By permission of the Estate of J. M. Barrie.

Beachcomber: From *Morton's Folly* (1933). Reprinted by permission of Sheed & Ward Ltd.

John Betjeman: 'Parliament Hill Fields' and 'Thoughts on "The Diary of a Nobody" ' from *Collected Poems* (1979); from *First and Last Loves* (1952) and from *London's Historic Railway Stations* (1972). Reprinted by permission of John Murray (Publishers) Ltd.

James Bone: From *The London Perambulator* (1925) and *London Echoing* (1948). Reprinted by permission of Jonathan Cape Ltd., for the Estate of James Bone.

Russell Brain: From *Tea With Walter de la Mare* (1942). Reprinted by permission of Faber & Faber Ltd.

Asa Briggs: From *Victorian Cities* (originally published by Odhams Press Ltd.). Reprinted by permission of the Hamlyn Publishing Group.

Thomas Burke: From *London In My Time* (Rich & Cowan, 1934). Reprinted by permission of Hutchinson Publishing Group Ltd.

Ford Madox Ford: From *Ancient Lights* and from *Return to Yesterday*, collected in *The Bodley Head Ford Madox Ford*, Vol. V. Reprinted by permission of The Bodley Head. From *The Soul of London* (Haskell House, Publishers Ltd., 1972). By permission.

A. G. Gardiner: From *Leaves in the Wind* (1920). Reprinted by permission of J. M. Dent & Sons Ltd.

Ira Gershwin: *A Foggy Day* (lyrics). Copyright © 1937 by Gershwin Publishing Corporation. Copyright renewed, Assigned to Chappell & Co., Inc., International Copyright Secured. All rights reserved. Used by permission.

Douglas Goldring: From *South Lodge* (1943). Reprinted by permission of Constable Publishers.

Stephen Graham: From *London Nightt* (1925). Reprinted by permission of The Bodley Head.

Graham Greene: From *Ways of Escape* (Bodley Head, 1980/ Simon & Schuster, 1981). Copyright © 1980 by Graham Greene. Reprinted by permission of Laurence Pollinger Ltd., Simon & Schuster, Inc., and Lester & Orpen Dennys, Ltd. (Canadian publisher).

Thea Holme: From *Chelsea* (Taplinger Publishing Co., Inc., 1971/Hamish Hamilton 1972). Copyright © 1971 by Thea Holme. Reprinted by permission of the publishers.

ACKNOWLEDGEMENTS

Molly Hughes: From *A London Child of the 1870's*, by M. V. Hughes (1934). Reprinted by permission of Oxford University Press.

Rudyard Kipling: From *Something of Myself*. Copyright 1937 by Caroline Kipling. Reprinted by permission of A. P. Watt Ltd., for The National Trust and Macmillan, London, Ltd., and of Doubleday & Company, Inc.

Stephen Leacock: From *My Discovery of England*. Copyright 1922 by Dodd, Mead & Co., Inc. Copyright renewed 1949 by George Leacock. Reprinted by permission of The Bodley Head, Dodd, Mead & Co., Inc., and McClelland & Stewart, Toronto.

Charles E. Lee: From *The Piccadilly Line: A Brief History*. Reprinted by permission of London Transport.

Richard Le Gallienne: From 'A Ballad of London'. Reprinted by permission of The Society of Authors as the literary representatives of the Estate of Richard Le Gallienne.

Rose Macaulay: From *Told By An Idiot* (Collins) and from *Coming To London* (1957). Reprinted by permission of A. D. Peters & Co., Ltd.

Sir Compton Mackenzie: From *Sinister Street* (1913). Reprinted by permission of Macdonald & Co. (Publishers) Ltd.; extract from *Echoes* reprinted by permission of The Society of Authors as the literary representative of the Estate of Sir Compton Mackenzie.

H. V. Morton: From *The Heart of London* (Methuen, 1925). Reprinted by permission of Associated Book Publishers Ltd., and A. M. Heath Ltd., for the Estate of the late H. V. Morton.

George Orwell: From *Coming Up For Air*. Reprinted by permission of A. M. Heath & Co. Ltd., for the estate of the late Sonia Brownell Orwell and Martin Secker & Warburg Ltd., and Harcourt Brace Jovanovich, Inc.

R. G. G. Price: From *A History of Punch* (Collins, 1957). Reprinted by permission of A. P. Watt Ltd., for the author.

J. B. Priestley: From *Angel Pavement* (1967) and from *London End* (1968). Reprinted by permission of William Heinemann Ltd.

V. S. Pritchett: From *London Perceived* (1962). Copyright © 1962 by Harcourt Brace Jovanovich, Inc. Reprinted by permission of Chatto & Windus Ltd., and Harcourt Brace Jovanovich, Inc.

C. H. Rolph: From *London Particulars* (OUP, 1980). Reprinted by permission of David Higham Associates Ltd.

Siegfried Sassoon: From *The Weald of Youth*. Copyright 1942 by Siefried Sassoon. Copyright renewed 1969 by Hester Sassoon. Reprinted by permission of George Sassoon and Viking Penguin Inc.

Bernard Shaw: From *Love Among the Artists* and *The Star*. Reprinted by permission of The Society of Authors on behalf of the Bernard Shaw Estate.

Edith Sitwell: From *Coming to London* (Faber, 1957). Reprinted by permission of David Higham Associates Ltd.

Logan Pearsall Smith: From *More Trivia*. Copyright 1921 by Harcourt Brace Jovanovich, Inc., renewed 1949 by William Hereward, Charles Rollo and Geoffrey Bridgwater Williams. Reprinted by permission of Constable Publishers, and Harcourt Brace Jovanovich, Inc.

Bernard Spencer: 'Regent's Park Terrace' From *The Collected Poems of Bernard Spencer*, ed. Roger Bowen. Copyright © Mrs Anne Humphreys 1981. Reprinted by permission of Oxford University Press.

ACKNOWLEDGEMENTS

Sir John Squire: From *A London Reverie* (1928). Reprinted by permission of Macmillan, London and Basingstoke.

Frank Swinnerton: From *Autobiography*. Copyright 1937 by Frank Swinnerton. Reprinted by permission of Tessa Sayle.

Patrick Waddington: From *Turgenev and England* (1980). Reprinted by permission of Macmillan, London and Basingstoke.

Stanley Weintraub: From *The London Yankees* (1979). Reprinted by permission of W. H. Allen & Co., Ltd.

H. G. Wells: From *Tono Bungay* and from *Love and Mr. Lewisham*. Reprinted by permission of A. P. Watt Ltd., for the Executors of the Estate of H. G. Wells.

Frederick Willis: From *A Book of London Yesterdays* (1960). Reprinted by permission of J. M. Dent & Sons Ltd.

Edmund Wilson: From *Europe Without Baedeker*. Copyright © 1947, 1966 by Edmund Wilson, renewed 1975 by Elena Wilson. Reprinted by permission of Farrar, Straus & Giroux, Inc.

P. G. Wodehouse: From *Lord Emsworth and the Girl Friend* (Barrie & Jenkins, 1935), and from *Psmith In The City* (1910). Reprinted by permission of A. P. Watt Ltd., for Lady Ethel Wodehouse and Hutchinson Ltd., and of Scott Meredith Literary Agency, Inc.

While every effort has been made to secure permission, we may have failed in a few cases to trace the copyright holder. We apologize for any apparent negligence.

The illustrations in this book were taken from the following sources: A. E. Daniell, *London City Churches* (London, 1895); E. T. Cook, *Highways and Byways in London* (London, 1903); Richard Doyle, *Manners and Customs of Ye Englyshe*, from *Punch* (1849); Augustus J. C. Hare, *Walks in London*, 2 vols. (London, 1878); Wilmot Harrison, *Memorable London Houses* (London, 1890); Phil May, *Fifty Sketches* (London, 1898); *Pictorial Half-Hours of London Topography* (London, 1851).

Index

In Berkeley Square